Single-Session
Therapy

Moshe Talmon

Single-Session Therapy

Maximizing the Effect of the First (and Often Only) Therapeutic Encounter

Jossey-Bass Publishers

San Francisco • Oxford • 1990

SINGLE-SESSION THERAPY
Maximizing the Effect of the First (and Often Only) Therapeutic Encounter
by Moshe Talmon

Copyright © 1990 by: Jossey-Bass Inc., Publishers
       350 Sansome Street
       San Francisco, California 94104
         &
       Jossey-Bass Limited
       Headington Hill Hall
       Oxford OX3 0BW

Library of Congress Cataloging-in-Publication Data

Talmon, Moshe, date.
 Single-session therapy : maximizing the effect of the first (and
often only) therapeutic encounter / Moshe Talmon.
  p. cm. — (The Jossey-Bass social and behavioral science
series)
 Includes bibliographical references and index.
 ISBN 1-55542-260-8
 1. Single-session psychotherapy. I. Title. II. Series.
RC480.55.T35 1990
616.89'14 — dc20   90-36407
                CIP

Manufactured in the United States of America

The paper in this book meets the guidelines for
permanence and durability of the Committee on
Production Guidelines for Book Longevity of
the Council on Library Resources.

The epigraph on the first page of Chapter One is an excerpt from "Little
Gidding" in *Four Quartets,* copyright 1943 by T. S. Eliot and renewed 1971
by Esme Valerie Eliot, reprinted by permission of Harcourt Brace
Jovanovich, Inc.

For information about our audio products, write us at:
Newbridge Book Clubs, 3000 Cindel Drive, Delran, NJ 08370

JACKET DESIGN BY WILLI BAUM
FIRST EDITION

Code 9067

The Jossey-Bass
Social and Behavioral
Science Series

Contents

Foreword

Surveys of outpatient psychotherapy have repeatedly found that most patients stay in treatment for a very short time. Many patients come for only a single session, and the average number of sessions is only three to six. It is widely assumed that patients drop out early because they are dissatisfied with the treatment they received. A closer look at dropouts from all forms of psychotherapy, however, reveals that most patients who quit after a single interview do so because they have accomplished what they intended and that, on the average, such patients report as much improvement as those who stay the prescribed course.

These findings present a problem for most schools of psychotherapy, which assume that successful psychotherapy requires considerable time. Hence, improvement after a single session must occur before the postulated therapeutic mechanisms have had time to work. Rapid improvers, therefore, have received relatively little attention from researchers and practitioners.

In *Single-Session Therapy,* Moshe Talmon, by refreshing contrast, has seized upon and developed the implications of improvement after a single session, and he has succeeded in specifying at least some of the features of a single therapeutic contact that contribute to this outcome. His central assumption is that most outpatients, by virtue of the fact that they are functioning in the community, have considerable powers of spontaneous recuperation, as well as ability to resolve their problems. The therapist can mobilize these latent potentials in single-session therapy, empowering the patient by showing understanding of his or her problems and symptoms and offering alternative solutions and encouragement. A further assumption is that almost all patients belong to a social network and that interaction with other members of that network may contribute importantly to the patients' distress and disability and, by the same token, to their therapeutic progress. Hence, when possible, another member of the network, typically a family member, should be involved in the therapeutic interview.

Finally, Talmon assumes that, since humans are thinking creatures who rehearse encounters in anticipation, interpret the meanings of encounters while they are transpiring, and mull over their implications in retrospect, therapeutic processes may be operating not only during the official treatment session but for as long as the patient is mentally in contact with the treatment situation. Therapeutic processes may start at the moment when the patient decides to make an appointment, continue during the initial office or clinic contact, and persist for an indefinite time after the treatment session. Therefore, intake and follow-up interviews are integral parts of single-session therapy.

Talmon's presentation of single-session therapy is convincing. His style is exceptionally clear and refreshingly free of jargon. He makes no exaggerated claims, and his points are amply illustrated by clinical examples and supported by systematic empirical findings from his own experience and the relevant literature.

The reader should be cautioned that single-session therapy may not be as easy as the author makes it sound. Although rightly giving the patient the lion's share of credit for the outcome of therapy, Talmon may be underestimating his own contributions. He is an astute and highly experienced therapist who has mastered a variety of therapeutic modalities, enabling him to be highly flexible in selecting the therapeutic maneuvers that will best fit particular patients. His experience also helps him select and focus on the problem or symptom most amenable to therapy, offer interpretations and suggestions at moments when they have maximum impact, and express these interventions in terms such that the patients will hear them as empowering and supportive rather than implicitly critical. These techniques are examples of subtle aspects of therapeutic encounters that the experienced therapist utilizes intuitively, and this may be important if not crucial to therapeutic success. Readers should not overlook the author's explicit recognition that, while perhaps as many as four-fifths of psychiatric outpatients receiving single-session therapy respond favorably, the remaining one-fifth, as well as most in-patients, require considerably more treatment.

Single-session treatment raises some disquieting questions about the organization of psychotherapeutic services — questions that have special pertinence in these times of heavy demand for psychotherapy coupled with shrinking financial support. To what extent do psychotherapeutic schools overestimate the psychopathology and underestimate the spontaneous recuperative powers and problem-solving abilities of most patients seeking psychotherapy? As a result, how much are psychotherapeutic facilities and personnel overloaded with patients upon whom are foisted more psychotherapy sessions than they need or want? To what extent does this possible misuse of available resources unnecessarily increase the cost of these services and restrict access for those who really need longer therapy? Talmon's persuasive demonstration that the preponderance of psychiatric outpatients benefit markedly from a single therapeutic session (plus intake and follow-up) should encourage the restructuring of psychiatric outpatient services so as to enable psychotherapists to spend less time on patients who do not need long-term psychotherapy, thereby freeing more time for those patients who do.

Because of its important implications for the theory, practice, and provision of psychotherapy, *Single-Session Therapy* should be read and pondered by all outpatient therapists, funding agencies, and organizers of psychotherapeutic outpatient services.

June 1990   Jerome D. Frank
                                       Professor Emeritus of Psychiatry
                                       Johns Hopkins University
                                       School of Medicine

In memory
of my parents
Pnina and David Talmon

Preface

Single-session therapy (SST) might be considered the ultimate of brief therapies. However, this book is not written for brief psychotherapists only. Apparently, all therapists have had single-session therapies and will continue to have them by plan or by default. Single-session therapy is defined here as one face-to-face meeting between a therapist and a patient with no previous or subsequent sessions within one year. As such, SST is the most frequently used length of therapy.

How, you might ask, could anybody be seriously helped in one session? Single-session encounters, you might argue, should be considered as no treatment at all or as intake or consultation at best. How could it be called therapy if therapy implies deep and long-term changes of personality? I was trained to see therapy as a relatively long process, and my own therapy terminated only after several years. Originally, the very idea of therapy lasting for only one session struck me as incredible. It took hundreds of single-session cases and two years of research for me to fully appreciate the therapeutic potential of the first and only session. In this book I give the information and experience that changed my view. I often use the terms *therapy* and *patient,* since most of the cases took place in a psychiatric clinic of a medical center and were treated by clinical psychologists with patients seeking psychotherapy. Other terms, such as *counseling, psychiatric consultation,* and *clients,* may be interchangeable.

The problem to date is that single sessions too often prompt the labels of "no-show" (for the second appointment), "dropout," "premature termination," "failure," and other negative or derogatory assignations. *Single-Session Therapy* shows how to use single sessions to prompt substantial changes in patients' lives. It explains how to capitalize on it, plan for it, and change normal therapeutic practices in order to support more creativity as well as effectiveness; it provides guidance on how to use time differently, how to foster readiness and motivation, and how to combine the necessary intake-diagnostic process with that of promoting change.

This book is not about how to condense five or twenty sessions into one; rather, it shows how to make what is already there a useful and positive therapeutic experience. The single-session-therapy approach is offered to patients and therapists who are ready and motivated to take care of business *now,* and it leaves the door open to what has become known as intermittent therapy throughout the life cycle.

Single-session therapy is as old as psychotherapy. The publishing of this book at this time is the result of rapid change in the reality of psychotherapy practice. The increase in health care costs necessitates a search for more cost-effective treatments, even as consumers are looking for less dependency on doctors and drugs (including prescribed medications) and more reliance on self-help and natural products. At the same time, the number of lucrative solo private practices in a fee-for-service setting that offer open-ended therapy is shrinking rapidly.

Single-Session Therapy presents twenty-one case examples of therapy with individuals, couples, and families. The age range of patients in these cases is from four to sixty-four years, and the presenting problems vary from those of the "worried well" who seek reassurance to those of patients who suffer from depression, anxiety, obesity, adjustment to divorce, family violence, and other problems. The therapeutic techniques range from simply listening and supporting patients' strengths to offering hypnotic suggestions, practicing solutions experientially, and giving dynamic interpretations. Single-session therapy may employ any of a wide variety of therapeutic techniques so long as the approach is tailored to the individual; however, SST is not useful for every patient. The book suggests criteria for inclusion and exclusion of potential SST clients. It discusses SST failures and ways to guard against undertreatment and possible premature termination.

Overview of the Chapters

Chapter One introduces the phenomenon of single-session therapy and reviews briefly the research base for this book as well as the available literature on the topic. Chapter Two focuses on the presession contact and how to set change in motion from the moment the patient calls to seek help. It suggests ways and criteria for identifying potential candidates for SST as well as those who are not likely to benefit from SST.

Chapter Three offers step-by-step guidelines for conducting effective single-session therapy with a variety of examples and presenting problems. Chapter Four explores two key concepts that underline the success of SST: first, empowering patients (and the ways in which therapists can restore their sense of autonomy, confidence, and independence) and, second, emphasizing the ways in which the natural process of change can assist the therapeutic process.

Chapter Five provides a slightly abridged transcript of an SST dialogue with a thirty-year-old patient. The commentary and follow-up show how the different principles discussed earlier are put into practice. Chapter Six discusses cases of SST failure (when therapy terminates prematurely) and suggests some of the lessons to be learned from them.

Chapter Seven discusses how therapists' attitudes determine their thoughts, feelings, and actions in therapy and suggests useful attitudes in working with single-session patients. Resource A provides the format of a brief, follow-up interview, which was used in the SST study. Resource B contains practical suggestions for managing time and money in order to meet the challenge of today's realities and to maximize the therapist's benefits from SST.

Acknowledgments

This book, although written by me, is the product of many people's work. First and foremost, I wish to thank my SST patients. Through their use of single-session therapy, they allowed me to help many more patients than I ever imagined possible. They taught me a great deal about a variety of human conditions and struggles I would never have known about had I stayed in the safe environment of private practice in my own neighborhood and within my own socioeconomic group. Early in my career, I traveled great distances to watch and learn from master therapists; but it was my SST patients who finally taught me who the real and powerful heroes of psychotherapy are: the patients themselves.

I wish to thank Steve DeShazer and Insoo Berg, who were the first to realize the value of this kind of therapy. They spread the word about it in the United States and Europe before I ever published or presented publicly anything about single-session therapy. Steve later introduced me to Gracia A. Alkema, senior editor at Jossey-Bass. I could not have asked for more. Gracia's graceful guidance and support throughout the project made the writing of this book a truly pleasurable challenge. She has a unique ability to make one's raw ideas clearer yet richer. I am grateful to my friends and colleagues who reviewed the manuscript and made many helpful suggestions: Donald Bloch, Steve DeShazer, Esther Elitzue, Joel Elitzue, Eyal Megad, Pazit Sela, and John Weakland.

For the clinical guidelines and many of the case examples, I am indebted to my partners in the single-session psychotherapy research project, Michael F. Hoyt and Robert Rosenbaum. They let me watch and follow up many of their cases and consulted with me on some of mine. Our individual and clinical differences made this project much more rewarding. While I was writing this book, we coauthored one article and made presentations at several conferences together. Chapter Three was cowritten with Michael and Robert, and Chapter Five was cowritten with Michael. The plural *we,* when used in this book, refers to Robert, Michael, and myself. We wish to thank the

Sidney Garfield Memorial Fund for providing partial support for the study.

I wrote *Single-Session Therapy* while holding a full-time staff position at the Kaiser Permanente Medical Center in Hayward, California. I enjoyed collaborating with a stimulating and competent team of physicians, nurses, psychologists, and social workers, who gave a new and truthful meaning to the term *interdisciplinary team approach.* In particular, I wish to thank my chiefs, Norman Weinstein and Paul Opsvig, who gave me all the room and support I needed for the writing of this book. My colleagues Wesley Lamb and Jane Brooks contributed important ideas regarding presession intervention and always agreed to back up my clinical duties while I took the time to complete this book.

I am especially grateful to my wife, Iris, for carrying more than her load in our life while I was writing this book. She was my closest friend and collaborator in getting the job done. I owe this book to her.

Berkeley, California   Moshe Talmon
May 1990

The Author

Moshe Talmon has studied the phenomenon of single-session therapy while working as a clinical psychologist at the Kaiser Permanente Medical Center in Hayward, California, and as a private practice consultant in Berkeley. He has also served as a reviewer, assessor, and consultant to Managed Health Network.

Talmon gives seminars on single-session therapy in the United States, Europe, and Israel. In addition to teaching and supervising psychotherapy at the University of Pennsylvania, the Tel Aviv University, and the School of Psychotherapy in Haifa, Israel, he is a former director of the Kibbutz Child and Family Clinic in Hadera, Israel.

Talmon received his B.A. degree in psychology from the Tel Aviv University and both his M.A. degree in experimental psychology and his Ph.D. degree in clinical psychology from the University of Pennsylvania. He was a research associate and teaching fellow at the University of Pennsylvania and the Philadelphia Child Guidance Clinic.

Talmon is married to scriptwriter and video producer Iris Yotvat and is the father of two.

Single-Session Therapy

One

When the First Session
Is the Only Session

> We shall not cease from exploration
> And the end of all our exploring
> Will be to arrive where we started
> And know the place for the first time.
> — *T. S. Eliot (1943)*

Therapist: Good morning. This is Dr. Talmon from Kaiser in Hayward. I saw you for a single session a year ago regarding your children.

Patient: Oh, yes. How are you?

Therapist: Fine, thank you. I am calling as a follow-up. You might remember that when you called us your two kids had severe behavioral problems, in particular your son, Jaimy, who was acting out every day, and you felt overwhelmed.

Patient: That's right!

Therapist: How are the children doing now?

Patient: They are doing very well. I did not have any problem with them since the one session we had. I sure remember how overwhelmed I felt at the time. The children were getting under my skin. Spending five years being a mother twenty-four hours

1

a day made me quite isolated, and I felt that I was the only mother in the world who had such severe problems with her kids.

Therapist: Is there anything you remember from the session?

Patient: I remember the session very well. Now, every month I have two appointments with myself for two hours each time. First I go out to do my nails, and then I usually meet with a friend in a café, and we chat for an hour. If I feel that the children begin to get under my skin, I simply take a break. Sometimes I just take a short walk. Other times I simply move to the next activity instead of staying stuck in a vicious circle with them.

Therapist: What do you think caused the change in the children's behavior?

Patient: By taking your suggestion, I began to realize that no one can be a mother all the time. We all need breaks and space for ourselves. When I took the time for myself, the children stopped getting under my skin. Then I started to feel better as a mother, which in turn freed me to take better care of myself (my looks, my diet). When I started to feel better about my looks and myself, my marriage turned to the better, and then my husband became more considerate and involved with parenting too. So, as you can see, a small change turned out to be quite a big one.

Therapist: Thank you so much for your input. It is very valuable for me, and I am certainly happy for you. As a therapist I feel it is mostly you who deserve the credit for the changes. After all, it is you who decided that you had had enough and needed to do something about it. It is you who knew your kids so well and were able to communicate clearly to me about it, so that I could come up with a useful suggestion. Last, but not least, you have translated what I said in such a nice and effective manner, so that you and actually your entire family could benefit from your action.

Patient: Thanks! It sure is nice to hear that from your doctor.

This is the transcript (slightly condensed) of one of the very first phone calls I made in an attempt to follow up with my patients who had dropped out of treatment after the first session. In retrospect, I realize that giving this mother the credit for the changes and taking a "one-down position" (Haley, 1963) in my role as a therapist was not a planned strategic move but rather the result of a genuine feeling on my part. I must confess that when I decided to make these follow-up calls to all my single-session patients, I was filled with worries. I thought that the patients would not remember me or the session. I feared that they would tell me what a poor therapist I was and how I had messed up their lives. I imagined them telling me what wonderful therapists they had found to repair the damage I had done.

The Paradox of SST and Psychoanalysis

To the best of my knowledge, the "founder" of single-session therapy (SST) was none other than Sigmund Freud, better known as the founder of the longest form of therapy, psychoanalysis. At the end of the nineteenth century, Freud treated a patient known as Katharina in a single session during one of his vacations on an Austrian mountaintop (Breuer and Freud, [1893] 1944). Later, he reported to have cured the composer Gustav Mahler's impotence during a single long walk in the woods (Freud, 1960). (I suspect that Freud cured Mahler's impotence in a single session simply because that was all that the time and situation allowed for; if Mahler had made a regular appointment for psychoanalysis with Freud and had come to his office, he probably would have spent quite some time lying on Freud's couch, and his impotence would have become an interesting case for further discussion. Freud was not terribly interested in the cost-effectiveness of his talking cure.)

While social agencies and overcrowded and understaffed community mental health clinics are the providers most likely to promote SST, most of the cases of successful SSTs reported in the literature were handled by therapists utilizing psychoanalytical concepts. For example, Grotjahn (1946) described a successful SST of a forty-five-year-old depressed physician. When seen two years later, the patient expressed gratitude for the insight he had gained and reported a stable and satisfactory home and work life. Being a psychoanalyst, Grotjahn attributed the success of the therapy to its having brought into consciousness repressed conflicting emotions. He was also able to provide some direction and advice, which the patient was readily able to accept.

In the context of the orthodox American psychoanalytical society of the 1940s, reporting such cases and giving directions to patients in the first session were very courageous. Grotjahn's report appeared in *Psychoanalytic Therapy: Principles and Application* (Alexander and French, 1946); in his autobiography, Seymour Sarason (1988) describes this book and the psychoanalytical community's reactions to it: "What they assert is that, under certain conditions, certain people with certain problems can, relatively quickly, sometimes in even one session, experience marked changes that endure and which are not predictable from theory. That book was as disconcerting to the analytic community, practitioners and theorists, as if the Pope had announced his conversion to Islam or his assent to abortion. It quickly became a nonbook in that community" (p. 320). Yet sporadic accounts about the value of SST continued to appear. For example, Saul (1951) reported in *Psychoanalytic Quarterly* the successful SST of a hypochondriacal woman, claiming that she was tremendously relieved in one interview and was given a key to the handling of future difficulties.

Of particular interest in the area is the work done by the psychoanalyst David Malan and others during the 1960s in London's Tavistock clinic, one of the bastions of psychoanalysis (Malan and others, 1968, 1975). Between 1962 and 1966, Malan and his associates followed forty-five "untreated neurotic patients" with various symptoms of depression, anxiety, impotence, frigidity, and ego dystonic homosexuality who were seen for single-session consultations and either dropped out or were considered unsuitable for psychodynamic therapy. They were followed up two to nine years after their therapy. Of those who had been interviewed by a psychiatrist no more than twice in their whole lives (most of them had been interviewed only once), 51 percent were judged to have improved symptomatically and 24 percent psychodynamically. Malan found that single-session patients "are of extraordinary interest, providing not only direct evidence of therapeutic mechanisms in everyday life, but also, quite unexpectedly, evidence about the therapeutic effects of single interviews" (Malan and others, 1975, p. 110). He concluded: "Clearly psychiatrists who undertake consultations should not automatically assign patients to long-term psychotherapy or even to brief psychotherapy, but should be aware of the possibility that a single dynamic interview may be all that is needed. . . . Finally, dynamically oriented psychiatrists should also be aware of the powerful potential therapeutic effect both of telling a patient that he must take responsibility for his own life, and of reassuring him that he can manage without therapeutic help" (p. 126). (A detailed case example and the therapeutic mechanisms used by the Tavistock's "untreated" patients are described in Chapter Four.)

My interest in single-session therapy grew out of my observations during two periods I spent as a psychologist visiting the United States from Israel. I started my studies of psychology and psychotherapy in the European tradition, seeing psychology as part of a philosophy of life dominated by psychoanalytical theories. Later, I had more versatile training in psychodynamic, family-system, cognitive, behavioral, transactional analysis (TA), and Gestalt modalities. I practiced psychotherapy for twelve years and was myself in long-term therapy with a Jungian analyst. In all that time, none of my teachers, supervisors, or colleagues ever mentioned, even in passing, that therapy may start and end in a single session.

I first visited the United States in the 1970s to study family therapy at the Philadelphia Child Guidance Clinic, where I faced the reality of poor single-parent mothers and their children. Girls did not have to *imagine* the Electra complex; they actually were molested by their fathers and other relatives again and again. Children did not struggle with separation and individuation; they struggled merely to survive in a world of poverty and physical and mental abuse. What was most bewildering to me was that while the problems were very real and rather horrendous, most patients used therapy in a very brief and crisis-oriented manner. They forced me to be brief, focused, and practical. In that context, psychoanalysis became a fascinating intellectual game of very little use in everyday practice.

Once back in Israel, I developed a private practice working in the affluent area of Tel Aviv and with members of the kibbutz society, which allowed me to resume the sense of working through lifelong problems with an intimate and long-term approach, primarily with individuals. I was a privileged listener, struggling with my clients through the hardships of life and empathizing with their deep need for personal and spiritual growth. I supported their separation and individuation from parental and cultural imprinting. I enjoyed the stability and intimacy of such a practice. Today, I must admit that that kind of therapy was not necessarily the most effective and useful to my clients, but it certainly supported my own growth and income in a lucrative profession.

I came to the United States once again in 1985, this time to California. Here, in contrast with the natural habitat of private practice at home, I was faced with the new reality of health care in America, with its surplus of providers and the growth of brief therapy in health maintenance organizations (HMOs), preferred provider organizations (PPOs), and employee assistance programs (EAPs). I learned that the growing national attention to the stresses of divorce, child abuse, and drug addiction is bringing to treatment many new patients who are not psychologically minded and who lack the time and resources required for long-term therapy. As a foreigner in this new environment, I developed an anthropological approach and tried to listen to and observe each family as if they came from another planet. Indeed, families from the Far East and Mexico often presented a whole new world to me. Once I was able to put aside my ego and biases, I was privileged to learn new and fascinating ways in which families and individuals struggle to solve their problems with very little intervention or help from me.

I learned about the frequency of the SST phenomenon by coincidence. About a year after I started to work in the Department of Psychiatry at the Kaiser Permanente Medical Center in Hayward, California, I entered the office of the department chief, Norman Weinstein, to discuss a complicated case. While waiting for him to finish a phone conversation, I noticed on his desk a package of computer printouts headed "Number of visits per patient, reporting period for prior 12 months." Each page presented a bar chart showing the pattern of practice of a single therapist. I asked Dr. Weinstein if I might look at the printouts. "Oh, sure," he replied. "I only read them occasionally now. I ordered them eight years ago, shortly after I became the chief here, and the results are almost the same every year. Here, take it all." I left his office carrying a bunch of computer printouts about the pattern of practice of some thirty psychiatrists, psychologists, and social workers.

When I studied the data, I was astonished by what I found: (1) the modal (most frequent) length of therapy for every one of the therapists was a single session, and (2) 30 percent of all patients chose to come for only one session in a period of one year. Many were offered another appointment but, even when no fee (or a very small one) was involved, they chose not to keep their second appointment or to seek therapy elsewhere. I later studied 100,000 scheduled outpatient appointments during a five-year period (1983–1988) and found the frequency of SSTs to be extremely consistent.

The data I analyzed in the computer printouts revealed that the therapeutic orientation of the therapists had no impact on the percentage of SSTs in their total practice. For example, a senior psychologist who had been trained in traditional psycho-analysis and who still had an analyst's couch in his office saw 48 percent of his clients for a single session. A social worker using object-relations theory saw 55 percent of her clients for one time only. A psychiatrist with a strong belief in the biological basis of mental illness saw 50 percent of his patients only once in the course of a year. I have worked with these professionals quite closely and know them to be competent therapists who are devoted to their patients. The percentage of therapists' single encounters with patients is somewhat higher than the percentage of actual SSTs since they may see patients in crisis or for consultation and refer them for further therapy with another therapist. If a patient continues therapy with another therapist, it should not be considered as an SST but rather as an assessment and referral.

Frequency of SST in Various Settings

As I later learned from a review of the literature, the high frequency of single-session therapy has been well documented over a period of more than thirty years in a variety of settings. Kogan (1957a, 1957b, 1957c) examined the records of all new clients in the Family Services Division in New York for a one-month period in 1953. Out of 250 new cases, 141 (56 percent) were closed after one interview. Spoerl (1975), examining the records of a mental health clinic serving a private HMO, found that 39 percent of the 6,708 clients seen in 1972 made only one visit to the clinic, despite full financial coverage for the first ten visits. Bloom (1975) studied the mental health service delivery system, both public and private in Pueblo, Colorado, for a two-year period (1969–1971) and found that 32 percent of 1,572 first-admission outpatients were seen for an SST. Although it is generally assumed that patients seen privately are more likely to engage in long-term therapy, Bloom found no difference in the frequency of SSTs between the public and private systems in this community. And Koss (1979) found the dropout rate in a sample of private-practice patients to be consistent with that seen in the clinical population. Baekeland and Lundwall (1975) did an extensive review of patients dropping out of treatment and concluded that in general psychiatric clinics, 20 to 57 percent of the patients fail to return after the first visit. In Prince William County, Virginia, the Community Mental Health Services sees 80 percent of the patients for a single session (Rita Morano, personal communication, 1989).

Dropouts or Miracles?

After reviewing the statistics on SST, I decided to look into somewhat more subjective variables, and so I asked the therapists at Kaiser to comment on some of their own SST cases.

They viewed their patients who did not show up for a second appointment as dropouts and described them with such terms as "resistance," "borderline personality," "not ready for psychotherapy," or "lack of motivation for change." When asked to comment about their success in the session, the therapists assumed that they had failed to create rapport with the patients or that the patient had not liked what the therapist had to say or offer. In analyzing therapists' evaluations of 141 SSTs, prepared at the time of the cases' termination, Kogan (1957a, 1957b, 1957c) found that in the majority of cases, therapists attributed unplanned terminations to client resistance or lack of interest.

The psychological literature has many references to dropouts from treatment but very few to planned SST. Most researchers focus on the negative side of this phenomenon. For example, Baekeland and Lundwall's (1975) review cites 330 references to dropping out of treatment. A "dropout" patient is described as "apt to deny his illness, to be resentful and distrustful, and to have sociopathic features" (p. 748). The therapist of dropout patients is described as "less experienced, more ethnocentric, dislikes his patient or finds him boring . . . less personable, lacks warmth and was more likely to assign them a poor prognosis" (p. 761).

Intrigued by what I had found, I decided to call all of the patients whom I had seen for a single session (often an unplanned one). In spite of my fears about what I would hear, the results of my follow-ups seemed almost too good to be true: 78 percent of the 200 patients I called said that they got what they wanted out of the single session and felt better or much better about the problem that had led them to seek therapy. A "blind" postdoctoral student interviewed a sample of my SST patients to reduce the obvious "demand characteristics" (Orne, 1969) created by the therapist following his or her own cases. Her interviews did not evoke significantly more positive or negative outcomes than my own interviews. Those who experienced no change gave mostly "reality" explanations as to why they did not return to therapy, such as "only morning appointments were available, and I couldn't take off from work." Only 10 percent did not like the therapist or the outcome of the ses sion. This also confirmed Kogan's (1957a, 1957b, 1957c) study, where follow-up interviews with SST clients revealed that reality-based factors that prevented continuance and improvements in the problem situations accounted for a substantial proportion of the unplanned terminations.

Bernard Bloom (1981), of the Department of Psychology at the University of Colorado, Boulder, has conducted the only detailed study on the therapeutic process of planned SST. He saw ten SST clients in a local community mental health center for two-hour interviews. All cases were satisfactorily concluded, with an open door for clients to come back if there were a need. Bloom called his clients two months later and found that all were doing well, nearly all had found the intervention helpful, and only one had sought additional help. He summarized his findings as follows: "Single-session encounters between mental health professionals and their clients are remarkably common. Not only is their frequency underestimated, but more importantly, their therapeutic impact appears to be underestimated as well" (p. 180). Though Bloom's study, with its small number of subjects and very primitive type of evaluation, may have little scientific value, his extensive review of the literature and the clinical guidelines he proposes are useful for all practitioners treating individual adults.

Silverman and Beech (1979) studied dropouts in a community mental health center and concluded that "The notion that dropouts represent failure by the client or the intervention system is clearly untenable. Almost 80 percent of the clients interviewed reported that their problem(s) had been solved, 70 percent reported satisfaction with the services rendered, and the majority of client expectations of the center were met" (p. 240). Littlepage and others (1976) studied the relationship between the number of a patient's contacts with a mental health center and the patient's evaluation of services. They found that the so-called dropouts evaluated services as highly as patients who reached "normal" termination. Nevertheless, most therapists continue to see their single-session clients in an unplanned manner and regard them as dropouts. In many cases, these encounters are not even recorded.

Therapists who have reviewed or analyzed successful SST tend to emphasize their own theories. For instance, Malan attributed the patients' genuine improvements to dynamic factors (insight, working through, and self-analysis), while others overemphasize the role of the therapist or the therapeutic impact. In his follow-up of 141 SST cases, Kogan (1957a, 1957b, 1957c) interviewed both the therapists and the patients. The therapists consistently underestimated the unplanned SST patients' (dropouts') improvements and consistently overestimated how helpful they had been to planned SST patients; two-thirds of the patients in both groups felt that they had been helped. Psychologist Nicholas Cummings and psychiatrist William Follette, working in the Kaiser-Permanente Medical Center in San Francisco, found that patients seen for only one session of psychotherapy resulted in a significant decline of the patients' overall utilization of medical facilities. This was evident over a five-year period. They admitted that "The findings that one session only, with no repeat psychological visits, could reduce medical utilization by 60 percent over the following five years, was surprising and totally unexpected" (Cummings and Follette, 1976, p. 167).

SST and Psychodiagnosis

Many therapists have been trained in accordance with the medical model, which views the first session as diagnostic, and therefore devote the first session or even the first few sessions to intake, assessment, mental status examination, and psychological or psychiatric testing. Naturally, if the purpose of the first session is assessment, therapists focus on gathering information and taking history. Unfortunately, this often means that they focus on diagnosing the correct disorder and fail to explore areas of strength; focus on the past more than on the present or the future; and, having to cover a wide variety of information, focus on content rather than process, making it difficult to create a focal point or main theme. Recently, I have been asked to review inpatient hospital stays for the Managed Health Network Inc. Talking to the attending psychiatrist or psychologist three or four days after a patient's admission, I have asked about the treatment plan and the progress made. The treating doctors have usually replied that they were still in the diagnostic phase and therefore unable to report any progress or treatment plan.

Other therapists, trained in interactional, social, or humanistic models, believe that the purpose of the first session is to create rapport with the client. Thus, they devote that session to getting acquainted, avoiding confrontation, challenges, or therapeutic interventions aimed at bringing about change. However, given the current concern about the possibility of malpractice suits, therapists these days are apt to focus on homicidal and suicidal thoughts or psychotic processes and to pose questions about physical or sexual abuse as well as drug and alcohol abuse. Naturally, when the content of the first session revolves entirely (or mostly) around those subjects, the patient is not very likely to leave the session with a sense of hope, relief, or positive thinking and may see the therapist's role as that of an investigator who uncovers dark secrets that then have to be reported to the "proper authorities."

The Three Types of SST

1. *Mutually agreed SST*—when both therapist and patient are aware of the possibility of SST from the very beginning of their interaction and mutually agree at the conclusion of the first session that SST is sufficient. This form of SST is clearly the most desirable, yet the least known in research and clinical practice.

2. *Patient initiating SST*—when the therapist plans a longer treatment and schedules a second appointment, but the patient elects to terminate therapy. This outcome can happen when the patient does not show up or does not call to cancel the appointment without rescheduling. This is the most common form of SST and least desirable from the therapist's point of view.

3. *Therapist initiating SST*—when the therapist does not schedule another appointment, although the patient might feel the need for more sessions. There are many cases in which practitioners might effect this form of SST. For example, the therapist

views the presented problem as "a normal problem of life" or as a problem that is not psychological in nature, and does not offer another appointment, while the patient resists the urge to challenge the therapist's diagnosis and walks out feeling untreated. In another scenario, the therapist views the problem as truly insolvable and sees no point in further sessions, although the patient still hopes for a solution or attributes magic power to the therapist and leaves the session feeling rejected. At other times, the therapist leaves an open door for the patient to call back, but a passive or extremely dependent patient might wait for the therapist "to read his mind" and might end up feeling abandoned. This is the least known form of SST and it has not been previously studied. Nevertheless, it is the least desirable from the patient's point of view and deserves more research and attention from therapists.

A Formal Study of Planned SST

When I first told my colleagues that 78 percent of the patients that I had seen for a single session reported "improvement" or "much improvement," some of them suggested that this positive outcome was probably due to the fact that most of the identified patients were children who had been treated in the context of their families: "Kids just grow out of most problems, and treating them with their families provided you with a natural cotherapist who did the job for you." Others said, "This is just crisis intervention and not real therapy." It became clear to me that therapists have much more difficulty accepting the phenomenon of SST than do their patients. I felt that there was a need for a formal study to test these arguments and learn more about the process of SST, and I consequently embarked on such a study with two other therapists who work exclusively with adults—Michael Hoyt and Robert Rosenbaum.

Each of the three therapists participating in the project had more than ten years of wide clinical experience. While all three of us are clinical psychologists, we had very different styles and backgrounds. Robert Rosenbaum, a chief psychologist at Kaiser in Hayward, California, is very active in the movement toward psychotherapy integration. Originally trained psychodynamically, he now utilizes a variety of modalities but particularly favors the systemic-strategic Ericksonian approach. He is currently working on a project to use musical principles to explain the psychotherapeutic process. As he is also a neuropsychologist who has seen the intractability of some brain-damage cases, he was the most skeptical of the collaborators at the start of the project. One day, Rosenbaum was walking in the mountains, indulging his doubts on the subject: "Perhaps some change can happen in a single session, but surely not a significant change. A lasting change requires the gradual processes that mold mountains: time, slow erosion, wind and rain sculpting the face of the stone over and over again." At that point, the trail turned around a bend. A huge avalanche chute came into sight. Half of a mountain, it seemed, had slid down into the valley last winter, changing both mountain and valley forever, all in the course of less than thirty seconds. As the project progressed, Rosenbaum's healthy skepticism became a very creative force, and he turned out to be the most effective therapist in the project.

Michael Hoyt did his predoctoral internship with Carl Whitaker and followed it with a two-year postdoctoral training program in short-term dynamic psychotherapy practice and research. Hoyt's interests include family therapy, existential therapy, and, most recently, redecision therapy (a form of TA–Gestalt therapy). He has ten years of experience at Kaiser, where he is the director of adult services in the Hayward psychiatry department. He agreed to serve as the principal investigator in our project.

In order to learn how to increase the likelihood that SST would be a mutually useful experience for both patients and therapists, Hoyt, Rosenbaum, and I decided to attempt planned SST with sixty patients, mostly individual adults, appearing for noncrisis, routine appointments. We submitted a formal research proposal to the Sidney Garfield Memorial Fund, stressing the relevance of our topic to the issues of cost-effectiveness and quality of care, issues of great concern to any good HMO. The fund agreed to support a one-year study.

In regard to our therapeutic style, Hoyt is usually very direct in therapy, while Rosenbaum is usually indirect. I like to use presession telephone conversations and to take time-outs during the first session (as I describe in Chapters Two and Three), while Hoyt rarely does it. I get much more accomplished in the first session if three or more members of the family attend, while Rosenbaum and Hoyt prefer to work with individuals or couples. In most of my cases, the identified patient was a child or an adolescent, while Hoyt's and Rosenbaum's patients were adults. In the end, we agreed to support each other's different styles rather than try to develop a universal SST, a "one-size-fits-all" treatment.

As our study was centered on exploratory investigation, we decided to conduct the study in the least intrusive manner possible and in as similar a manner as possible to the regular ways of delivering service in our clinic. Only ten of the sixty sessions were conducted in the presence of one or two other therapists, who usually watched the session from behind a one-way mirror. Although most cases studied for this book were seen in a regular fifty-minute session by a single therapist, the sixty attempts at planned SST should be viewed as an exploratory study and not as an attempt to conduct well-controlled laboratory research. (The effect of the one-way mirror and the impact of the team on the patients and the outcome of SST could be the subject of a separate study.)

For evaluation we used the standardized intake form used in our clinic, which is completed by the therapist at the end of each session. We developed a protocol for follow-up interviews to be administered to the patients (over the phone), by someone other than the therapist, three to twelve months after the session. The follow-up interview form that we used is presented in Resource A. A few of the questions used are similar to ones used by Gustafson (1986) in his brief therapy study.

The sample for the study was heterogeneous rather than highly restricted and well controlled. It consisted of regular intake patients assigned to us randomly and included whites, blacks, Hispanics, and Asians with problems ranging from those of the "worried well" looking for reassurance through depression, insomnia, panic attacks, adjustments to divorce, family violence, and others. The patients ranged in age from four to ninety-three and in education level from Ph.D.-holding professionals to high school dropouts. Patients who would not ordinarily be seen as regular intake patients in our clinic were excluded from the SST sample. These consisted of patients who were actively psychotic, suicidal, or in severe crisis (usually seen in our department on an emergency basis, the day they call); patients calling for medications (seen by a psychiatrist); and patients calling because of drug or alcohol problems (seen in the Department of Behavioral Medicine, which has a separate team from that in our clinic).

Of the sixty patients in our sample, we were able to reach fifty-eight for follow-up interviews. Of those fifty-eight, thirty-four (58 percent) did not require additional sessions — that is, patient and therapist mutually agreed at the end of the session that no further appointment was required but left an open door for the patient to call whenever necessary. Those patients had had no further contact with us or any other therapist until they were called for a follow-up, three to twelve months after the session. Of all the SST patients contacted, 88 percent reported either "much improvement" or "improvement" since the session (on a five-point scale, where 1 = much improved, 3 = no change, and 5 = much worse, the average level of improvement was 1.7); 79 percent thought that the SST had been sufficient, with an average satisfaction rating of 1.6 (again on five-point scale); and 65 percent reported having other positive changes that were clearly unrelated to the presenting problem and might be attributed to a ripple effect. The SST patients showed slightly more improvement and more satisfaction than the patients who were seen for more therapy, but the differences were not significant. Three patients reported no improvement or felt that SST had not been sufficient, and they received further therapy.

In order to compare our findings with other clinical populations, I asked Mordecai Kaffman (1990), the medical director of the Kibbutz Child and Family Clinic in Israel, to conduct a retrospective study of the length and outcome of the cases he treated in his kibbutz. Kaffman is a very thorough psychiatrist with thirty years of clinical experience. He keeps detailed notes on all his cases. He lives in a small and stable communal community of 635 people and can easily obtain objective feedback from patients treated at various points over a long period of time. Kaffman analyzed 211 cases and obtained follow-up sessions three to six years after the initial session. Sixty-four cases (30 percent) were seen for SST. The rest required short-term therapy (defined as up to eight sessions — 41.5 percent) or long-term therapy (28.5 percent). Kaffman usually devotes four to five hours to his initial session in order to obtain a reliable diagnosis and plans on intervention with a whole network of people who may influence the outcome. Kaffman obtained follow-ups from the patients, as well as from the referring source (like the nurse, the personal physician, the teacher, or the parent). The reported improvement of the SST patients averaged 1.4 (on the same five-point scale used in our study). In 84 percent of the sixty-four SST cases, Kaffman was able to reach a planned and mutually agreed SST.

Regardless of the determined purpose of the first session or the therapist's expectations as to the necessary length of therapy, patients take something out of the first session and often decide that it is sufficient for them at that time. With SST, patients can move quickly back to the business of life, and they are much more likely to own their solutions and changes without getting stuck in a long process of patienthood, where naturally more dependency is likely to develop. As for the therapist, the challenge created by the common phenomenon of a single session is to learn how to be aware of it, plan for it, and maximize its unusual potential.

Two

The First Phone Call:
Presession Screening
and Preparation

In all beginnings dwells a magic force
for guarding us and helping us to live
So be it, heart: bid farewell without end!
— *Herman Hesse ([1943] 1969)*

The moment a patient picks up the phone to call a therapist or a clinic, therapy has already begun. The patient has recognized a problem and taken action (making the phone call). It is useful to seize that very moment. The presession conversation and the time between the initial call and the first session are important parts of SST.

In my work in a busy, large medical center, I found that the rate of no-shows was greater among patients who were provided immediate appointments following emergency calls than among those who were scheduled for routine appointments (usually two to three weeks after the call). In addition, those who waited for an appointment were more likely to show improvement than those who did not. At one point when our waiting-list time had reached six weeks, I volunteered to call patients who had been waiting for an appointment. I realized that spending just ten to fifteen minutes on the phone enabled me to screen the cases better — to determine, for example, which cases might need higher priority and should not wait, which patients just needed reassurance or referral elsewhere, and so on. When I thought I could be of further help, I scheduled an appointment at the end of the phone conversation. The information I got over the phone combined with the time elapsed till the first session gave me an important perspective on how the problems evolved (and sometimes resolved) over that period of time. Sometimes I asked the caller to call me forty-eight hours prior to the session; of those patients, one-third called to inform me that the problem was greatly improved and that they did not need the appointment anymore. I usually suggested that they come in anyhow so "we can better understand what made the change possible and plan for relapse prevention."

When I began making these presession phone calls, I refrained from any interpretations or suggestions over the phone, feeling that without further observation I was very likely to make mistakes. After several dozen cases, I tentatively started experimenting with very minimal and benign interventions, along the line of what Steve DeShazer (1985) calls "skeleton keys." When an anxious patient called me and I wanted more information before the first session, I would say, "Between now and our first session, I want you to notice the things that happen to you that you would like to keep happening in the future. In this way, you will help me to find out more about your goal and what you are up to." This comment contains several messages: (1) The therapist is interested in natural and effortless changes ("notice the things that happen to you"). (2) The focus is on the transition from the present to the future ("Between now and our first session," "that you would like to keep happening in the future"). (3) The patient is active and soon can assume a "one-up position" ("In this way you will help me").

It is desirable to call the patient back within twenty-four hours of the initial call. This is not only a matter of courtesy. Between 30 and 40 percent of first appointments with mental health professionals are not kept, especially in public settings (Palmer and Hampton, 1987). This results in loss of money and time and increased negative feelings for the therapist and the clinic. The initial phone call is likely to establish the pattern of the first session. The therapist can use it to set the stage for a productive session.

Tamara Levy (1989) modified a standard telephone intake procedure in a counseling center in Los Angeles by adding a few questions such as: "What else is stressful in the family?" and "Who else is involved with the family who could be helpful to counseling?" She ended the conversation by saying, "Therapy is most effective if all those involved come in at least for the first session. Who will attend?" The vast majority of callers are women, and an attempt to get other members of the family in the first session is often a struggle, which Carl Whitaker (Whitaker and Keith, 1981) called "the battle for structure." One might expect such demands to increase the no-show rate, but Levy found that using the above questions reduced pretherapy dropouts, increased participation of family members and significant others, and altered the orientation of both patient and therapist so that they viewed the problem in a larger context.

Kaffman (1990) used a more elaborate presession procedure. He requested that prior to the session the patient as well as others (like the referring source, personal physician, parent, teacher, or employer) submit in writing their answers to three questions:

1. What are the central issues (or problems) in the eyes of the respondent?
2. What are the factors (or circumstances) that seem related to the issue (or contributed to the problem)?
3. What measures have been used so far in an attempt to solve the key issues?

Kaffman takes half an hour to an hour to review the answers as well as other medical and psychological reports. He says that his clinical work in the kibbutz taught him that the specific problems of the individual or the family indeed intertwine with and are influenced by the surrounding organizations to a significant degree. Therefore, he tries to include at least the most important people in the human ecological system with which the referred patients and their families are in close daily contact. Kaffman's high percentage of effective and planned

SSTs may be related to the extra time and bigger number of people he involves in preparing for the session and the intervention.

Who Should Come for the First Session

Mrs. Jones called the clinic at the advice of her daughter's pediatrician. She told the receptionist that Belinda, her twelve-year-old daughter, had been suffering from diarrhea and abdominal pains for more than a year and had missed so much school as a result that she had been expelled. The mother was routinely asked who else lived in the house. Mrs. Jones had been divorced for three years and lived with Belinda and her fifteen-year-old son, James. The father lived in a nearby town. The therapist assigned to the case chose to schedule his own appointment in order to decide who should be included in the first session. If the main problem was in school, the therapist might include the schoolteacher, principal, and counselor. If the problem was primarily physical, the therapist might invite Belinda's pediatrician, who worked with him in the same medical center. The referral source is an important part of the therapeutic system. As the pediatrician had referred Mrs. Jones to the clinic, the therapist called him first.

Therapist: You recently referred to us the case of a twelve-year-old girl, Belinda, with abdominal pain. Her mother, Mrs. Jones, called today to seek therapy. Do you recall the case?

Pediatrician: I sure do, and I am very glad her mom finally called you, because I am at my wits' end. I have seen her over twenty times this year and ran every test I could think of. You can read it in her medical chart. They all came back negative.

Therapist: Do you think that she is medically "clear" at this point?

Pediatrician: All I can say is that she was referred to me because gastrointestinal problems of children are my specialty, but I could not find anything. I referred her to an allergist, and he tried a new diet and medication, with no results.

Therapist: Would you be interested in joining me for the first session with the family?

Pediatrician: If you insist, I will come, but to tell you the truth, I have had it with this case. Every time I see her name again on my schedule, all I can say is, "Oh, no! What did I do to deserve that?" In my opinion, she has a severe case of hypochondria, and it is primarily psychological.

Therapist: Let me first call Belinda's mom, and if I need your help in the session, I'll call you back.

Pediatrician: God bless you and good luck. If I don't hear from this girl for a whole month, this will be just a miracle.

Next, the therapist called Belinda's mother.

Therapist: This is Dr. Talmon from Kaiser in Hayward. I gather you called us today regarding your daughter Belinda.

Mother: That's right.

Therapist: Do you have a few minutes to talk with me now?

Mother: Yeah, this is a good time. Belinda is in her room reading, and James is in school.

Therapist: I was asked to see you since I am an expert in helping children and families solve problems. What I have in front of me is the description of the problem you gave to the receptionist this morning. I also took the liberty of calling Dr. Cohen, who referred you to our department, and I briefly reviewed her medical chart.

Mother: I am glad you did that, since Dr. Cohen knows my daughter very well, and by now she must have a thick chart. She was born at Kaiser in Hayward, and I always took her there. I know Dr. Cohen does not believe she has a medical problem, but I believe her pains are for real.

Therapist: I understand. When you called, you mentioned the abdominal pains and Belinda being suspended from school. At this time, what is your main concern?

Mother: Right now I am mostly worried about school. She missed so many days, she might never catch up. The school assigned her last week a home teacher who comes here a couple of times a week. I am so worried. Education is so important, especially for a black girl.

Therapist: What seems to be the problem in school?

Mother: That's what puzzles me. She used to like school. Most of her friends are there, she liked her teacher, and she is an intelligent girl and used to have good grades. This is why I think she really has a medical problem. Otherwise, she would have gone to school. I kept nagging her about it, but it seems the more I do it, the less she goes to school.

Therapist: It sounds like it has been very difficult for both of you. Is there anybody else who is aware of your calling us today or who is worried about Belinda?

Mother: Only Belinda is aware that I called you. Her brother once in a while gets upset with her staying at home all day. I am sure her father loves her, but since the divorce it's me who takes care of the kids' medical and school problems.

Therapist: Do you think they might care enough about Belinda to come in for the first session?

Mother: I really don't know, since we've never got together as a family since the divorce.

Therapist: I know how much you want to help your daughter. The best way I know to help the situation is to get everybody in the family, including Dad and James, so I can get everybody's ideas about it. Now, would you like to invite Belinda's dad yourself, or would you like me to do it?

Mother [after a long silence]: I guess I should try first, and if he refuses, I will let you know.

Therapist: It sounds like we have a deal here. How about next Wednesday at 6 P.M.?

Mother: That's fine. Thank you for taking the time to talk with me today. I will see you Wednesday.

Therapist: Thank you for calling us today. I am looking forward to seeing all four of you.

In the initial response to the patient's call, the therapist tried to convey the following messages: (1) I care. (2) I listen. (3) I take my professional responsibilities seriously. (4) I treat your individual needs respectfully.

Accomplishing one small step in the right direction in the presession phone conversation is plenty. This therapist usually tries to broaden the therapeutic system as much as possible and include as many potential "change agents" as possible. In this case, he started with the idea that he might want to include the pediatrician and/or school representatives in the initial session. He decided against it, however, since his impression was that numerous attempts had already been made by the doctors and the school to resolve the problem. Inviting these people might create just "more of the same," or what the Mental Research Institute group (Watzlawick, Weakland, and Fisch, 1974) describes as solutions (such as school conferences or medications) that become part of the problem. The therapist tentatively ruled out school trauma or learning disability as part of the problem and tried to create a therapeutic system that might introduce new dimensions. He took a clue from the mother's statement that the family had never got together since the divorce to suggest that the father should be included. Since in this case the father still lived nearby, neither of the parents had remarried, and Mrs. Jones had stated that she believed that Belinda's father loved his daughter and had agreed to call him, the therapist hoped to elicit his and Belinda's brother's help. (We will return to Belinda and her family in the next chapter.)

Presession Tasks

Some generic therapeutic tasks can be assigned prior to the first session. For example, when the presenting problem is an acting-out teenage boy and the complainant is the mother, the therapist can often hear on the phone that she is overinvolved with the boy in a vicious cycle, while the father is peripheral or out of the picture altogether. Described below is a presession assignment a therapist gave to the mother of a thirteen-year-old boy who defied her, talked back, did not do his chores, broke a curfew, and experimented with drugs. Notice how the therapist cultivates motivation and cooperation:

Therapist: I am willing to help you and your son, but in order to do so, I need your help between now and our first session. Would you be willing to do something different?

Mother: I'm so desperate, I'll do anything you say.

Therapist: I appreciate it. Yet I want you to take one moment to think about it, because it might be difficult for you.

Mother [after a short silence]. I am thinking to myself that it took me a very long time to realize that something is going wrong here, and an even longer time to overcome my self-pride and stubbornness in order to call for outside help. So I guess I am ready to do whatever it takes.

Therapist: Congratulations! I'm a father myself, and I can't even begin to tell you how long it took me to acknowledge that I could use a little help myself. What I'd like you to do in the ten days between now and our first session is to keep a very detailed diary of all your son's actions. I want you to write it down in a log. Do it right there and then, indicating the time and place and everything he does or says word by word. Do you understand why that is so important in order for me to help your son?

Mother: I am not really sure.

Therapist: I work with many teenagers, and what they very often do when they come to my office is act here very differently than they do at home, trying to convince me that the only problem is that Mom is nagging them too much. You know and I know that this is not the whole truth. In order for me to help him, I need to know the truth so I can get to the bottom of the problem. You probably know your son better than anybody else. Therefore, I want you to bring me this information, and I want it to be observed where things really happen naturally, which is at home.

Mother: I got it.

Therapist: I want to warn you that your son might try to pull you from doing your job. He will try to push your buttons in such a way that instead of writing it all down, you will be busy talking and arguing with him. You'll need to stick to writing down everything so I'll know your son the way he really is without any interference. Do you still think you can do it?

Mother: I will bring you a full diary of his actions.

Therapist: That's a promise. I'll see you all on Friday at 4 P.M.

While the content of the task is aimed at gathering more information about the problem, the therapist has already done some joining with the mother ("I am a father myself," "You know and I know"), as well as prescribing a structural change by offering the mother an opportunity to move from the reactor's role to the role of an observer. The therapist hoped that if she stayed busy writing the diary, she would not be able to get into the vicious cycle of action and reaction with her son.

What Should Be Avoided

When you know very little and have a very limited time, as with the initial phone call, what you choose not to ask or say is even more important than what you do ask. The therapist should keep factual and history questions to the bare minimum and avoid detours such as being overconcerned with the precipitating event, which the caller may wish to discuss for hours. While it is not always possible, the therapist may try (when time and cooperation allow) to get enough information to answer the following questions:

1. Am I the right person for this patient? If patients list many physical complaints or side effects from medication, they should see a physician and not a psychologist. If patients call in a depressed state and the therapist finds out on the phone that they drink excessively, the therapist should not see them unless the therapist or someone else in the facility is knowledge-

able about chemical dependency and can help the patient in detoxification. Too many therapeutic opportunities are wasted by patients telling their problems to several people before getting to the right person. One should be honest about one's limitations, work with a multidisciplinary team, and have a handy list of community resources. If it is done right, the initial phone call can save the patient much money and time. Furthermore, the first session is often critical. Patients who are mismatched or shuffled from one professional to another are likely to be turned off and drop out.

2. Who is my customer? There is very little chance of effective SST without a customer in the room. The customer is the person who is the most likely to do something different in order to solve the problem or to take the therapist's advice. A therapist who agrees to see individually a teenager referred by her mother, the school, or the police is likely to get just a visitor ("My mother sent me" or "I really don't know why I'm here"). In the initial session, therapists should try to include as many potential customers as they can. The caller may be one of them, since he or she was concerned and active enough to call. In order to identify all the potential customers, the therapist may ask the caller, "Besides you, who is most concerned about the problem? Who else do you recall having tried to help with the problem?"

Another way to find customers is to ask who in the system has the power to change the present situation. Too often, therapists see only the "victim" alone or with the complainer — for example, a child with a mother — while it is actually somebody else (the father or the teacher) who might "hold the strings." In Belinda's case, the therapist decided to broaden the therapeutic system and include the father and brother. In all the previous attempts to solve her problem, it had been the mother alone who had assumed the responsibility.

3. What is the hidden agenda, if any? If a mother calls the therapist with an endless list of problems regarding her kids, the therapist may ask her whether she is engaged in a custody battle with the child's father. When a patient is referred to psychotherapy after many visits to the emergency room or physicians

without any findings, the therapist should find out whether the patient wishes to change his or her workplace. Therapists should refer such patients to lawyers, mediators, family courts, or forensic psychiatrists. There is no point in trying to help people change themselves while their true agenda is to change somebody else, get money or time from somebody else, or obtain a verification of illness.

Who Will Benefit from SST

The above three questions raise a more generic one: Who is likely to benefit from a single session, and who should be excluded from the very beginning? This is a very simple and at the same time a very complex question. Therapists are not likely to know anything definitely until they call or see the patient for a follow-up after the SST. Therapists always work with partial knowledge, and as they gain more experience in diagnosis, they will feel more comfortable "knowing that they don't know." I myself continue to make many "false negative" mistakes in predicting who will benefit from SST. That is, I continue to underestimate patients' capacity to change now and become overconcerned by their seeming pathology and overwhelming problems. The SST therapist should be familiar with mental status examinations (Kaplan and Sadock, 1989; Korchin, 1976), initial psychiatric interviews (Gill, Newman, and Redlich, 1954), family initial sessions (Haley, 1987), and forming a *DSM-III-R* diagnosis (Spitzer, Skodol and Williams, 1988; Reid and Wise, 1989). At the same time, therapists may view psychodiagnosis with healthy skepticism. In the initial phone conversation, you can begin with a simple question to determine whether the patient is an SST candidate. It is simple, since it is usually patients who determine the length of therapy. Therefore, it is helpful to ask the patient as early as possible about their expectations:

- How and how soon do you anticipate the problem to be solved?
- How do you think therapy will help you to deal with the problem?
- What made you decide that now is the right time for therapy?

The answers to any of these questions provide an initial idea about the patient's expectations and readiness for change. If patients express a need to solve the problem now or "yesterday" (as they often do), the therapist can encourage this state of readiness. If patients feel that they need longer therapy, the therapist should go along with their request and encourage an explicit commitment to being an active and responsible participant in the therapeutic process so as to reduce the chance of a dropout. Naturally, the rate of no-shows is highest in the initial three sessions.

Patients who answer these questions with "I don't know" or some other vague or uncommitted response might turn to be negative responders or nonresponders to any length of therapy. From a cost-effectiveness point of view, it might be ideal to identify these patients in the very first session and let them go or refer them elsewhere.

To identify all potential SST candidates along diagnostic categories is an impossible (or at least a very complex) task, because SST patients vary widely in age, presenting problems, and *DSM-III-R* categories. Therapists should not expect to know from the initial phone contact who would benefit from SST. However, they should attempt to be aware of potential SST candidates from the very beginning. When I first tried to list SST candidates, I used a rather logical approach and listed the motivated, resourceful, insightful, and "worried well" patients with good support systems. I excluded all those with severe forms of mental and addictive disorder as well as chronic and long-standing problems. As we followed up 260 SST cases, the list of counterindications kept shrinking. For example, we were certain that long-term problems with severe symptomatology, such as cocaine abuse, panic, or character disorder, were all clear-cut counterindications for SST. In most of these cases, we automatically scheduled another appointment. During our follow-up, however, we learned that many of those patients used the session as a demarcation line — "That's it. Enough is enough!" — and left both problem and therapy behind. Our sample of successful SST cases included patients with problems such as daily cocaine use, depression, obsession, panic attacks, and separation, divorce, and violence in families. On the basis of our clinical and research experience, we could create only a preliminary list of inclusion and exclusion criteria.

We first defined who is not likely to find SST sufficient:

1. Patients who might require inpatient psychiatric care, such as suicidal, psychotic, or intoxicated patients.
2. Patients suffering from conditions that suggest strong genetic, biological, or chemical components, such as manic depression and schizophrenia.
3. Patients with clear neurological or brain damage (like dementia, Alzheimer's disease, or pervasive developmental disorder).
4. Patients who request long-term therapy up front, including those who are anticipating and have prepared for prolonged exploration of their development and sense of self. Patients who have had long-term therapy and either liked it or got used to it are not likely candidates for SST. For example, we had few mental health professionals as patients when we studied how to plan and conduct SST. They were interested in the study intellectually but did not consider SST to be sufficient for their needs.

Originally, the exclusion list included patients with a variety of Axis II diagnoses such as dependent, hysterical, narcissistic, and borderline personality disorders, because it was assumed that they would benefit only from long-term therapy. However, a few patients with character disorders did benefit from SST, but sometimes they were less pleased with it and felt abandoned. So, while borderline patients may not be satisfied with a single session, it can be a useful and cost-effective treatment for some of them. Two cases with personality disorders who were seen for a single session are discussed in detail in Chapter Four (Malan's case of a woman with passive-dependent hysterical personality) and Chapter Six (a patient with a borderline personality who wanted someone to take care of her but did not have clear symptoms or problems). Kaffman, in comparing all cases of SST, brief therapy, and long-term cases, adds the following disorders to the above list of exclusions from SST: anorexia nervosa, bulimia nervosa, attention deficit disorder, child pervasive developmental disorder, agoraphobia, hypochondriasis, and somatoform pain disorders (chronic pain).

Below is a partial list of patients who may be candidates for SST:

1. Patients who come to solve a specific problem.
2. The "worried well" who come for a mental health check-up essentially to ask whether they (or their significant others) are "normal."
3. Patients seen with significant others or family members who can serve as natural supports and "cotherapists."
4. Patients who can identify (perhaps with the therapist's assistance) helpful solutions, past successes, and exceptions to the problem that occurred prior to seeking therapy.
5. Patients who have a particularly "stuck" feeling (anger, guilt, grief, and so on) toward past events and are fed up with it.
6. Patients who come for evaluation and need referral for medication, medical exams, or other nonpsychotherapy services (legal, vocational, financial, religious, or similar counseling).
7. Patients faced with a truly unsolvable problem. Acknowledging the impossibility of change and aiding patients to cease useless or compulsive attempts to solve the impossible may help them attain a measure of equanimity and acceptance by letting go of futher treatment and attempts for "cure."
8. Patients who will be better off without any treatment.

Frances and Clarkin (1981) argue that the last category may constitute as many as 35 to 40 percent of psychotherapy patients who continue treatment although they have negative response or no response to therapy. Among negative responders, Frances and Clarkin include borderline patients with poor tolerance to the nature of the psychotherapy process and patients who enter treatment primarily to justify a claim for compensation or disability or to support a lawsuit. They suggest that nonresponders will include chronically dependent, treatment-addicted patients, patients with antisocial or criminal behavior, and patients with factitious illness. In terms of *DSM-III-R* disorders, Kaffman (1990) found that patients with adjustment disorders reacted most favorably to SST. In his sample, all nineteen adult cases with this diagnosis were treated with effective and planned SST. These patients exhibited maladoptive reaction to one or multiple identifiable psychosocial stressors, with symptoms such as disturbance of mood and conduct, physical and sleep complaints, inhibition at work or from studies, and increased interpersonal difficulties. Most of the stressors were located inside the family and fewer within the community or larger human ecosystem (like the army). Stressors included love affairs, bereavement, new marriages, remarriages, and problems at work or school. Interestingly enough, while many *DSM-III-R* disorders were treated effectively with SST, other cases with the same diagnosis (and severity) required a longer treatment. This category of disorders included anxiety, oppositional-defiant, obsessive-compulsive (child and adolescent) conduct, encopresis, enuresis, dysthymia, and obesity.

When Patients Call in Crisis

Dorothy, a forty-one-year-old divorced mother, called the clinic concerning fifteen-year-old Brian, her only son. Dorothy told the receptionist that Brian had threatened suicide and running away, and she felt it was urgent that she talk to a therapist the same day. The therapist on call that day called her back an hour later. She said that her husband had abandoned her two years earlier and since then had drifted away from his relationship with his son. "He is too busy for me," said Brian about his father. Recently, the boy's first girlfriend had dropped him, and that had precipitated the runaway and suicide threats. The therapist told her, "From what I hear you say, it sounds like your son needs some reassurance about your position as his mother. First, as a mother, you can listen to him and let him know that you understand how awful he must feel to be dropped by someone he loves. Second, as a mother and a responsible parent, you can let him know loud and clear that you are not going to tolerate any threats of running away and that you cannot live with the fear of him killing himself." Dorothy responded that she would pick Brian up at school in an hour and have a straight talk with him.

The therapist scheduled an appointment with Dorothy for two weeks later. Since suicide risk was involved here, he informed her of the clinic's crisis and emergency service in case she needed help before then and told her of the danger signs that she should watch for. A therapist who wished to feel more safe might see such a patient right away or hospitalize the patient. (The session with Dorothy and Brian is discussed in Chapter Three.)

As I pointed out at the beginning of this chapter, these phone conversations were already part of the therapy. Therapy starts before the first session and is likely to continue long after the last session. You cannot *not* communicate. Even when the therapist's answering service is the only presession contact, there are many therapeutic issues involved. How long did the phone ring before the patient was attended to? Was the patient put on hold? Was the patient asked how he or she could be helped or just asked for his or her name and phone number? Was the patient told who would call him or her back and when? The routine in our clinic is that the receptionist takes the initial information and schedules the intake. Many of the SST patients we followed up did not have a presession conversation with a therapist. When we analyzed the SST failures, we learned that some patients stated that they felt they had to wait too long, that they asked for a physician and got a psychologist, or that they were invited alone to work on a problem that was essentially interpersonal and required the presence of a spouse. Some cases where referrals were required after the first session could have been saved with an appropriate presession phone conversation.

When therapists perceive a presession contact as part of the therapy, they will find it easier to get down to business quickly instead of starting the first session from scratch or in a more formal and traditional manner. In the next chapter, we present step-by-step guidelines for SST.

Three

Effective
Single-Session Therapy:
Step-by-Step Guidelines

> If a person can turn from predicting illness to anticipating re-
> covery, the foundation for the cure is laid.
> — *Bernie Siegel (1986)*

This chapter addresses the questions of how to start and end
therapy in one session, how to create a focus when there is so
much information to sort out, how to open up toward patients'
strengths rather than pathology, how to use the first session to
practice solutions, how to leave enough time to attend to last-
minute issues, and what to include in the final feedback and
how to leave an open door for further change or therapeutic
contacts. It describes, step by step, how to conduct single-session
therapy, using case examples and verbatim reports of individuals, couples, and families.

Getting Started

The last chapter described how a presession telephone conversation can be used to induce and prepare for change. This

Note: This chapter was written with Michael F. Hoyt and Robert Rosenbaum.
They served as the therapists in four cases described in this chapter; Hoyt as
the therapist for Mary and Regina and Rosenbaum for Martha and Carla.

allows the therapist to start the session with a question about pretherapy changes rather than the traditional discussion about problems or information gathering. In fact, the therapist can start the session with this question even when there was no presession contact. Noonan (1973) followed up patients who called for an appointment but did not show up; 35 percent explained that their failure to show up was due to improvement between the time they called and the first appointment. To illustrate how the therapist can begin the first session, we will return to the case of Dorothy, whose fifteen-year-old son Brian ran away and threatened suicide. After greeting mother and son and making them familiar and comfortable with the setting, the therapist proceeded:

Therapist: You initially called us two weeks ago. What changes have you noticed in the last two weeks?

Mother: He and I had a talk, and since then, he has made some very definite changes. He follows the rules at home and school. He comes home when he is supposed to. He does his homework and chores. He is more cooperative and open with me.

Therapist: This is very encouraging. What have you done to make these changes possible.

Mother: I gave him an ultimatum. But first I gave him my support and love. I said to him that I understand the problems he is going through. About his relationship with his father, there is nothing I can do, and he will have to learn how to deal with his father. About his girlfriend, I said that I know how painful it is, yet I am sure he is going to have plenty of others. I laid down the rules and told him he has to straighten out his schoolwork. I made it clear that I cannot fix his problems with his father, and running away from it all is not an acceptable solution. I told him he has a choice to live with me and follow my rules or go to live with his father. If he does not want to live with his father and continues to break my rules, I will send him to military school, where he is going to have no choices. He has chosen to stay with me.

How could it be that following a single and brief phone call so much changed? Anybody who works with divorced families and suicidal teenagers would believe that that is simply not possible. If we had not videotaped this session and maintained a follow-up contact with this family for three years, we would not have believed it ourselves. Starting with the question "What changes have occurred?" conveys to patients the message that the therapist indeed expects changes and helps the therapist to pick up where the patient is at the time rather than assuming that the intake notes or medical chart are accurate and the situation is status quo. It also helps the therapist to quickly identify any worsening or disturbing problems. Patients are accustomed to talking with doctors about what is wrong and painful. Yet researchers have repeatedly found that rates of spontaneous improvement among patients receiving no treatment range from 9 percent with schizophrenics to 52 percent with most other patients (Endicott and Endicott, 1963), and a summary of seventeen well-controlled studies yielded a median spontaneous remission rate of 43 percent (Frances and Clarkin, 1981). Noonan (1973) followed up on patients who called for an appointment but did not show up; 35 percent explained that their failure to show up was due to improvement between the time they called and the first appointment. The fact that it is methodologically impossible to measure spontaneous improvement occurring within treatment should not stop us from exploring or even facilitating it in treatment.

Fostering Readiness to Change

Franz Alexander (1965, p. 102) argues that whether the therapy will be short or long really depends in the ultimate analysis on the ego's integrative capacity, not what kind of symptoms or syndromes the patient has. While Alexander's claim may be valid, it is still hard to measure "the ego's integrative capacity." We have tried to use the concept of readiness. Like Alexander's concept, the concept of readiness is somewhat vague. We conceptualize it as a state of immediate preparedness and willingness in which various conditions are near a threshold and can,

with recognition and skillful facilitation, be assisted and poten-
tiated into actuality. Readiness may occur when old mental con-
structs have either decayed "spontaneously" (through disuse or
maturation) or been actively proved untenable or unworkable,
resulting in a crisis with its attendant combination of emotional
pain and growth opportunity. In psychotherapy, readiness may
also help therapists recognize when a patient has already made
movement in one sector of the "psychological triangle" of think-
ing-feeling-acting but has not yet made the other changes necessary to restore congruence (Hoyt, Talmon, and Rosenbaum,
1990). Creating readiness for action and change is crucial for
the success of SST. What the therapist eventually chooses as
the final intervention largely depends on the patient's readiness.
In every stage, it is better to move with a small step or give
a very small task that the therapist is confident that the patient
is ready to carry out than a big task that might evoke fear and
ambivalence. But therapists who want to foster their clients' readiness to change must themselves be ready to be taken by surprise by their patients' capabilities.

Alternative Openings

Therapists can help patients to expect change now by introducing the possibility of SST right from the start, even in
cases where there has been no presession contact. When my colleagues and I conducted our study of planned SST, we experimented with various openings. Two versions that we found to
be effective are presented here (the third is presented as part
of the case study discussed in Chapter Five). One version is as
follows: "We have recently learned that one-third of the people
who come to therapy here do so for only one session and very
often find it to be helpful and sufficient. Yet I want you to know
that if today or at any point in the future you and I find that
further work is needed, I will be available and will be glad to
see you for more sessions. Is that okay with you? [pause]. Good.
Now, what is it that you would like to accomplish today?" Another version is: "We have found that a large number of our
patients can benefit from a single visit here. Of course, if you

need more therapy, we can provide it. But I want to let you know that I am willing to work with you hard today to help resolve your problem quickly, perhaps even in this single visit, as long as you are ready to start doing whatever is necessary."

These statements give a number of important messages. In the very first sentence, the therapist lets the patient know that change is possible. At the same time, the therapist leaves the door open for the patient to choose no change or more therapy. This seems to minimize resistance and dependent passive-aggression and also helps patients feel that any changes that they make are made autonomously rather than coerced. Telling patients of the therapist's intention and willingness to work hard with them is evidence of the therapist's sincerity and helps build trust and alliance. Finally, the therapist lets patients know that change is in their hands, that they are expected to be active participants.

Focusing on Pivot Chords

The therapist's next job is to find a focus for the session. Patients often provide the focus in their own words. It is rarely a deep-seated secret, so the therapist should not overlook the obvious. Sometimes, however, patients are in so much pain, confusion, and conflict that they are unable to sort it out.

The first element of a successful focus is its ability to carry a captivating metaphor that catches the listener's ear. Understanding how a pivot chord functions in music can be useful here. In music, the pivot chord is an ambiguous chord that contains notes common to more than one key and thus can imply several directions to the music and facilitate the transition from one key to another. Analogously, a central task of the SST therapist is to construe the patient's difficulty in such a way that it can function as a pivot chord for change (Rosenbaum, Hoyt, and Talmon, 1990). In the case presented below, the therapist talks with the patient in terms of her own view of the world. By using language and metaphors derived from her life and language, the therapist makes the patient feel understood and validated while at the same time offering a new perspective. The therapist may want to introduce some element of doubt or openness to alternative meanings in the patient's world view without denying the patient's experience or confronting it in a way that leads to resistance and a battle over which view of the experience is "right." Here is a case example of utilizing a pivot chord:

Martha, a very religious sixty-year-old woman, came in complaining of a driving phobia. She had been in a minor automobile accident a few months earlier, when she was grieving over the loss of her son who had died two years earlier. Martha had no previous psychiatric history. During the interview, she described a number of hardships (including losing other children) that she had courageously struggled with. Martha was determined to overcome this phobia and was using breathing and meditation exercises with indifferent success. She was forcing herself to drive to essential activities but was finding it hard to leave the house and drive to visit friends, go to the movies, or do other pleasurable things. Instead, she stayed home and worked on her embroidery. The therapist asked Martha how she would know when things were starting to improve, and she replied that it would be when she could get into the car and relax, not grip the wheel so tightly.

Here was an ideal opportunity for a pivot. The therapist had Martha demonstrate first how she clenched her hands anxiously while driving and then how she held and moved her hands while embroidering. Then he spoke to her: "Now, close your eyes and imagine you're anxious and scared and holding the wheel of the car. Grip the wheel really tightly. Very good. Now I'm going to ask you to do something difficult [since Martha was a woman who would rise to a challenge]. Keeping your hands the way they are, I want you to see your hands in your mind as they embroider. I want you to keep watching your hands embroidering with your inner mind and notice the pattern that unfolds as I speak to you about some things from which you can learn something important that can come in handy."

Hypnotic induction with hand levitation led into trance work. Sometimes the physical changes can be sufficient for a patient, but often it is useful to tie in a network of meanings.

For example, this patient was asked to visualize embroidering a pattern of fear. Once she had accomplished that, she was asked to embroider, on the same cloth, a complementary pattern of courage and faith. At the end of the session, she commented that she felt that the session had helped her work further on things that she was "already working on but hadn't quite realized it." It is useful to provide a pivot to a patient, but it is better yet if the patient provides the pivot for herself.

In looking for the focus, the therapist should listen attentively to the patient. Often patients will literally describe how the presented symptom serves a role or a purpose in their family or with significant others. For example, Carla, an overweight twenty-seven-year-old woman, requested hypnosis for weight control. Her self-esteem had declined recently, which she ascribed to her weight gain. Carla had never been in therapy and denied other difficulties in her life. She readily admitted, though, that at other times in her life she had had the same weight and felt more confident about herself. Carla mentioned almost in passing that she had recently moved back in with her mother, who was quite critical of her weight gain. When the therapist pursued the issue, she mentioned that her brother was a drug addict and stated, "I have always had the weight of being the ideal child." Although the patient did not make a conscious connection between her presenting problem and the burden of being the ideal child, the therapist perceived this as a focal statement with a capturing metaphor (or pivot chord, if your imagery is acoustic rather than visual). At this point, the therapist agreed to provide hypnosis for weight control, but only if Carla would agree to do something first: to alter her relationship with her mother. Since the mother was closely monitoring her, it would be impossible to just lose weight on her own. Instead, the therapist suggested that Carla should inform her mother of her plans to lose weight and post her daily weight on the family refrigerator, *but that she should lie* when she posted those figures. Carla was first shocked and then intrigued with the idea. Therapist and patient shook hands on this plan, and hypnotherapy for weight control was then provided. During the induction, indirect suggestions for autonomy were liberally interspersed with a method for finding the weight that she would find ideal.

A good focus can provide a leverage for a whole chain of changes. In Carla's case, the therapist provided a seemingly small but profound alteration (after all, ideal daughters do not lie to their mothers). This could serve as an opening to all sorts of changes.

Looking for Patients' Strengths

It is useful to possess various technical options, such as hypnotic suggestions, behavioral time-outs, thought stoppage, dynamic interpretations, circular questioning, positive connotations, and so on. But it is also desirable to keep these in reserve, listening carefully and openly rather than jumping the gun or putting the patient in the Procrustean bed of your theory of choice. To illustrate this point, we will return to the case of Belinda, the twelve-year-old with abdominal pains discussed in Chapter Two.

All four family members — Belinda, her divorced parents, and her brother — appeared for the first session. Considering the fact that nobody in the family had ever seen a psychotherapist before and that it was the first time that they had all met together since the divorce, the therapist chose to move very slowly and cautiously in the session. The issues related to Belinda's physical complaints and school avoidance were not discussed at first. The therapist maintained an open and low-key conversation and included everybody in the family. Although she was never asked about it, twice during the session Belinda insisted that her abdominal pains were real and that she would like to go back to school. The therapist listened attentively, said, "I believe you, Belinda," and moved on to the next subject. The therapist explored Belinda's strengths and interests and learned that she had a great attachment to animals. They had quite a zoo at home, including cats, a dog, turtles, a snake, and fish. She was particularly attached to a cat named Morris, which was very sickly. When asked who in the family had the hardest time letting go of the good times they had had when they all lived together, they shared some fun memories, and Belinda cried over the loss of the family unity.

In his concluding remarks, the therapist underlined a few things that had been said in the session and addressed each family member separately. He first turned to the father: "Considering the fact that your past disagreement with Mrs. Jones led to divorce, I particularly appreciated your ability today to communicate that you would leave it up to Mom how to handle Belinda, since she lives with her, and yet to express that you know how much work and hardship goes into raising two teenagers in a single-parent home." Then he turned to Belinda's brother, Jimmy, and said, "I heard you saying how much you would like to help your sister to go back to the normal, outgoing and happy person you know her to be. I don't know of a better way to do it than serving as an older brother role model who goes about his own life in that manner." The therapist listed a few age-appropriate independent activities that Jimmy could start to pursue. Then he turned to Mrs. Jones, praising her for her love and devotion to both of her children. He said that this family session today might never have come about without her persistence. He underlined her dilemma of being a devoted mother and yet, for financial as well as personal reasons, needing to pursue her career as a teacher. "Both of your children are clearly growing up, but this is a long process, and I don't know when you'll feel comfortable enough to pursue your career and spend more time with friends and doing other things." Last, the therapist turned to Belinda, saying, "I heard you when you said that you are very motivated to go back to school, but I still don't know when this is going to happen. One thing I'm sure of is that it will happen at the moment you are ready for it. Until then, I would strongly encourage you to stay at home and take very good care of Morris the cat, who seems to be sick and needs your care."

This was an unusual session for the therapist, since his main training in family therapy had been in the structural approach. He had spent three years at the Philadelphia Child Guidance Clinic with Salvador Minuchin, his mentor and supervisor. Minuchin's style is active and managerial. He runs a session in a decisive and often dramatic way, and one would never be mistaken about who was in charge of the session. Naturally, the therapist often followed his guidelines. His regular style with the Joneses would have been to be confrontative and use the session to induce intensity to unbalance the family system. At times, he might change the seating arrangements in the room, bringing the parents closer so that they could reach a decision about how to bring Belinda back to school and then giving the parents or the family as a whole his directives or tasks. Using a systemic approach, the therapist would typically conclude the session by addressing the family as a whole and prescribing a joint family task. In the case of the Joneses, the therapist did not do any of these things. Being an explorer with minimal intervention was a true change for him. It is possible to change therapeutic style if the therapist leads the session by following the patients' footprints.

Considering the severity and duration of the symptoms and the systemic-developmental issues, the therapist did not view the Jones family as good candidates for SST, and he offered them a second appointment, but they never reappeared. The following transcript of a follow-up phone conversation with Belinda's mother a year and a half later indicates that the SST had apparently provided a face-saving way out of the family impasse and that positive change begot other growth-sustaining changes.

Therapist: How is Belinda doing now?

Mother: She is doing much better. She goes to school and complains less about abdominal pain and diarrhea. She seems more enthusiastic about herself and life in general.

Therapist: What do you think made the change possible?

Mother: About a week after the session, she said she is tired of being sick and that she made up her mind to go to school. She still has occasional pains, but she insists on going to school with or without them. My feeling is that she thinks more positively and is more active. For example, she joined the volleyball team and became one of their stars.

Therapist: What do you remember from the session?

Mother: This one time we came in made a tremendous difference. It was the first time since the divorce that all of us sat together and talked. I was very surprised to hear that my ex-husband appreciated the work I have done for our daughter. I was proud of her when she said that your being a male and white did not matter to her and she judges people as humans [the patient was black, and the therapist had inquired whether she would rather talk to a black woman therapist]. This was an opportunity for all of us to open up more toward each other. I felt that after this session we continued to be more open toward each other, and in return Belinda was more open to us. I'm sorry we didn't show up for the next session, but I chose after we left to say to Belinda that from now on it's all going to be in her hands. I handed her your appointment slip and said that she can decide for herself if and when to seek professional help.

Therapist: Besides the specific issue of the physical complaints and the school avoidance, have there been other areas that changed for the better or worse, and, if so, what are they?

Mother: I think she chose to basically take better care of herself. For example, she groomed herself better, concentrated more on her schoolwork, developed new friendships, and became more dependable at home. As a result, I could become more positive toward her, and started to drop her little cards in her lunch bag or under her blanket, telling little things like how proud I am of her.

Practicing Solutions in the Session

As Belinda's case illustrates, validation, reassurance, and encouragement are important ingredients in therapy. Talking about a problem, meta-communicating, often gives patients the perspective and information necessary for them to move on. Sometimes, however, greater therapeutic impact is achieved if the patient has a here-and-now experience, rather than just a there-and-then explanation. A powerful experience in which the patient thinks, feels, and acts differently is a useful therapeutic tool. It moves the patient past the stuck point, it makes real and immediate the desired change, it creates a sense of freedom, and it helps to prove to patients the uncompelling nature of whatever considerations they were using to hold themselves back and stay stuck. Use of an experiential component in SST should not be limited to a particular technique or theory. Among the options available are in-vivo behavioral desensitization, psychodynamic transference confrontation, Gestalt two-chair work, visualization, imagery, and family sculpting. Below is an example of a therapist enacting in the session a ritual to bring about change in a particular painful experience and "stuck" feeling.

When Mary, a woman in her late twenties, was initially screened for psychotherapy, she mentioned a series of problems and then said, "What is really bothering me is something I have carried as a secret for years. My father molested me for a long time, when I was in my teens." She described a situation of terrible abuse and exploitation and made the connection between the sexual abuse and her subsequent low self-esteem and various personal problems. Mary had made repeated attempts as an adult to confront her father and discuss what had happened and her feelings about it, but each time he rebuffed and mocked her. In fact, he continued to make occasional attempts to exploit her, promising to loan her money but then withholding the loan unless she gave him sexual favors. "I am tired of this shit," explained Mary. "I want to put it behind me and be done with it. I want to get him and what he has done to me out of my life, once and for all!"

The therapist's main activity to that point had been to listen sympathetically (already a major change for the patient from what had occurred with her father). Now he decided to help the patient capitalize on her urgent sense of readiness and said, "You need a way of divorcing your father and breaking the bond, something that will make the break total and permanent for you. Some people might want to say certain words; others might burn pictures or do whatever means to them that they are free and done with him. You need to create a personal ceremony, one that will let you be free all the way through your mind and your soul. Spend some time thinking about what you want to do, and bring it in. We will meet in a week. Okay?" The patient liked the idea, and she agreed.

A week later, Mary arrived at the session with her husband, Jack, a portable stereo tape player, and an envelope. She looked nervous but said that she was ready. The therapist started the ritual by giving a brief speech, similar to that of a clergyman at a wedding but expounding on the significance of breaking away ("an ending, a separating, one voice becoming two from this day on," and so on). As the master of ceremonies, the therapist nodded to the patient to proceed, only occasionally directing, pacing, or pausing for emphasis and heightened impact.

The patient read aloud a several-page account of her betrayal and outrage, giving witness to what she had never before dared to reveal. While she read, her husband played songs about love and betrayal poignantly coordinated to her plaint. Several times she paused, overcome with emotion, and then continued. At the end of her reading, she pulled out from the envelope a picture of her father, along with a cigarette lighter. The therapist held the picture with a scissors while she lit the picture. Eerily, the father's face in the picture was the last portion to burn. The smoldering ashes fell into the office trash can, a glass of water was poured over the ashes, and for good measure and to the delight of Mary and Jack, the therapist spit into the ashes. They all laughed. Mary said that she felt free. Then she reached again into the envelope and pulled out several copies of a "Decree of Divorce" that she had written and had had professionally printed. It declared her "no longer the daughter of _____ except through biology." Mary signed each copy, as did Jack and the therapist. Jack then played happy music while Mary explained that she would frame one copy of the divorce decree to put next to her graduation diplomas, another copy was for her sister, and a third would be sent to her father. "The last time I will contact him," she added. The last copy was given to the therapist, who was honored to accept it.

Before closing the ceremony, the therapist asked Mary to close her eyes and to get a vivid picture of herself when she was a little girl, "before all the bad things happened." When she indicated having a clear image, the therapist asked her to keep that image and "now also see yourself as you are now, a strong grown-up woman." When she got that image, the therapist continued: "Now I want you to do two things. First, I want you to notice that you are now a grown-up, no longer a little girl, no longer vulnerable. You are strong now, an adult and capable of taking care of yourself. Now, in your mind's picture, see the grown-up you bend over and pick up the little girl and hold her close and lovingly. In a nice way, the little girl just sort of blends into you, and your arms are around yourself. And you know that she is safe inside of you and that you will always protect her." Tears ran down Mary's face. A few moments later, when she opened her eyes, her face looked beatific. She laughed freely, looked around, and hugged her husband. After a couple of minutes of celebration and expressing their appreciation, the session ended. No further therapy was sought.

Practicing solutions experientially in the first session can be used as a diagnostic tool to test the waters. If therapists entertain an idea or solution in the early part of the session, they can present it as a tentative solution in an "as if" or "let's pretend" way. As discussed earlier, timing the patient's readiness is crucial in SST, and therapists want to avoid conveying an evaluation or giving a prescription before the patient is ready to hear the diagnosis or to carry out the prescribed task. Using the "what if" or "let's pretend" scenarios early in the session not only will avoid solutions that were already tried and failed or met the patient's resistance but also will allow the therapist enough time to explore alternatives or reframe the problem in terms that the patient is more likely to accept.

Some schools of brief and active psychotherapy (such as the Milan group led by Mara Selvini-Palazzoli and the Milwaukee group led by Steve DeShazer) tend to delay the delivery of interventions or feedback to the last minute of the session. Our experience at Kaiser has been that trial interventions (including practicing solutions experientially) can be used throughout the session, and we have found that they are a very useful diagnostic tool as well as helping to refine the intervention and match it with the patient's readiness. An example is the case of Brian, a fifteen-year-old boy who threatened to run away and to commit suicide (discussed in Chapter Two). At the therapy session, to which Brian's father had been invited but which he did not attend, Brian and the therapist did role-playing scenarios of father-son conversations in which Brian expressed his feeling that his father had let him down and did not care for him, thus helping Brian to communicate his feelings directly and clearly.

Exercising tentative solutions in a "let's pretend" play can introduce some humor and playfulness into an otherwise grim situation. For the therapist, this is an opportunity to test the patient's motivation and cooperation in regard to the therapist's tentative ideas and solutions. Early in the session with Brian and his mother, the therapist tested the hypothesis that the patient ran away from confronting his father and his feelings about the divorce. When the therapist initiated a "let's pretend" telephone conversation where the patient was to confront his father about not calling or seeing him, the boy's voice during the play was weak and flat. The therapist tried to reverse the roles, having Brian act the part of his father, but his expression stayed very tentative and timid. At the end of the session, the therapist chose not to give him any assignments regarding his relationship with his father and instead concluded the session by congratulating Brian's mother for the presession confrontation with her son and prescribing basically more of the same of what had already worked. He then asked her whether she would mind if he had a brief talk alone with her son. She was very glad for the opportunity and left the room. The therapist briefly shared with the boy personal experiences of being dropped by girlfriends and suggested the "win-win game" for future dating, whereby he would ask a girl who he was sure would reject him for a date so that he could learn new ways of handling "stuck-up" girls without taking the rejection as a personal blow. They joked about tricks that boys use to get girls to want to date them. Finally, the therapist and the patient discussed a number of age-appropriate ways of differentiating from his mother without having to blow up (like staying overnight with a friend from a family that the mother knew and trusted, planning a week of outdoor camping during summer vacation). These were introduced only as examples rather than as a prescription.

Here is what Brian's mother reported at the six-month follow-up after that single session:

Interviewer: How is your son doing now?

Mother: He has improved a lot. He is not running away. He talks to me and tells me his feelings. He feels that his father had let him down. He is doing much better, his grades are better, and he is better with his friends.

Interviewer: How would people around him say he has changed?

Mother: One of his friends talked to me recently. She said he seemed a lot happier than he was before.

Interviewer: What do you think has made the change possible?

Mother: Before, I was scared. I wasn't pressing him, and I let him dictate to me. After I talked with you, and you said, "you've got to be his mother, he depends on that," I did just that and said to him that these are the rules of the house. I put my foot down, and then he sat down and started talking with me. That helped. I communicated to him that he cannot scare me by running away.

Interviewer: Besides the specific issues of running away and suicide threats, have there been other areas that have changed for better or worse? If so, what are they?

Mother: His schoolwork is better. He is getting closer with friends, and he has a steady girlfriend.

Interviewer: What do you remember from the session?

Mother: The doctor was very concerned and took the time to listen with both my son and myself. I was very impressed that he was able to pick up on how close my son and I are. Talking with him, hearing a professional viewpoint, I was able to set my mind at ease realizing that Brian's feelings were normal, and that took my fears away.

Allowing for Last-Minute Issues

The therapist can provide an opportunity for the airing of last-minute issues by asking, "Is there anything we did not cover at all today that you would like me to know about? Are there any questions you would like to ask me?" These questions should be raised early enough in the session that there will be time to include them in the formulation of the solution and the conclusion of the session. Often, only after those extra probes will patients come forward with the ultimate bottom-line question that brought them to seek help, such as when the "worried well" ask, "Doctor, please tell me the truth, am I crazy, or is what I'm going through just normal?" For example, Regina came to therapy several months after the death of her husband of many years. Friends had been trying to fix her up with another man, but she was not interested in dating. She missed her husband painfully and thought of him often, especially at mealtimes and at bedtime, and sometimes she did not sleep well. Near the end of the interview, when she was asked whether she had any other concerns, Regina anxiously described how she could almost hear her husband's voice once in a while, and she asked, "I'm not going crazy, am I, Doctor?" There were no suggestions of serious psychopathology, no history of psychiatric problems, and no family history of mental disorder. Regina had good social support and a variety of activities. The therapist was able to reassure her that she appeared to him normal and that she was undergoing the painful healing process called mourning. She could call back if needed, of course. She did not need additional therapy.

Giving Final Feedback

The final feedback usually includes four elements: acknowledgment, compliments, diagnosis, and prescription.

Acknowledgment. Regardless of how much the therapist and the patient have accomplished in a single session, it is important to acknowledge the reason that brought the patient to the session. Otherwise, patients might leave the session feeling that they had bothered the therapist for no reason and were stupid to worry about this and that. Worse yet, they might leave feeling unheard or misunderstood. In the acknowledgment, the therapist should try in one or two sentences to emphatically connect with the emotional state of the patient, or what Mann (1973) called "the present and chronically endured pain." Even in cases where no pathology or intervention is indicated, it is helpful to acknowledge the need for the visit as a periodic "mental health check-up" by caring and responsible people.

Compliments. The therapist should underline what has been learned about the patient's thinking, affect, and behavior that is useful in solving the problem. Even with the most severe problems and pathological situations, people do some useful things some of the time. Underlining the patient's positive qualities and strengths should not be done in a pollyannaish manner but rather as a way of providing a constructive bridge between existing strengths and resources and what the therapist is about to present as diagnosis and/or intervention. In this way, therapists can present their intervention as a small and rather natural next step in the right direction.

Diagnosis. Diagnosis (or assessment) is often presented not as a *DSM-III-R* label but rather as a reframing of the problem in solvable or autonomous terms. For example, an anxious patient might be told that he scares himself with imaginary thoughts of catastrophes, and a depressed patient might be told that she has been so loyal to her family that she sacrifices her own welfare. The reframing is put in positive terms to "capture the ear of the listener" (Gustafson, 1986) and cast in an autonomous language that helps the patients see their choices (Goulding and Goulding, 1979) and thus opens possibilities for responding differently.

Prescription (or Task). While therapists may entertain various fancy interpretations or solutions, in SST it is most useful to present patients with the smallest and simplest task that the therapist can come up with, worded to correspond with the patients' idiosyncrasies and world view. It takes a few years of humbling clinical practice to realize that the therapist's role is not to be smart or even to be right but rather to be helpful to patients through effective interventions.

A mother of a seven-year-old boy and a six-year-old girl called our clinic requesting therapy for her son. She said that following her second marriage six months earlier, the boy, who previously had been very close and open with her, had become angry and insecure at home and was presenting behavioral problems at school. All members of the new family, including the husband-stepfather, attended the session. Two therapists interviewed the family while a third observed from behind a one-way mirror in an observation room. During a consultation break near the end of the interview, the team noted many developmental and structural issues in the family, as well as various individual psychological problems. Away from the family, a lively and intellectual discussion developed among the three consultants, and several interventions were considered, ranging from a powerful interpretation regarding the oedipal rage of the boy to a clever and complicated strategic-systemic task designed to strengthen the newly formed alliance of the mother and stepfather while reducing the overinvolvement of the mother-son duo. These ideas, however, were not used. Instead, the therapists first acknowledged to the family members how difficult and sometimes confusing it must feel to go through so many changes in such a short period (in addition to the new marriage, in the past six months the family had moved to a new house, both spouses had started new jobs in a new career, and the kids had started at a new school, where they knew no one). The therapists then congratulated everybody and particularly the newly wed couple for surviving a difficult transition and the many changes that followed. The therapists mentioned how affectionate, open, and supportive of each other all family members seemed to be in the session. Individually, the therapists focused only on the stepfather, admiring his persistence and wondering how he would integrate himself into such a close-knit group (the mother had been a single parent for five years). They prescribed a once-a-week ballgame for the men in the family (the stepfather and the identified patient).

In a six-month follow-up, the mother reported, "My son is much improved. He trusts more, and he is much more affectionate and warm, especially with my husband. Since we have seen you, my husband has had to adjust to a lot. He now says, 'I feel really good being here with all of you.' Now, he feels he fits in."

During the final feedback, therapists can alternate among all four elements. For example, when the therapist has a very clear picture of the problem, he or she could start by formulating a constructive definition of the problem, from there go back to the compliments element, looking for the exceptions to the problem (the times when the patient coped with life without the problem), and then look for a link between the compliments and a possible solution. At other times, the therapist might first find a good idea for a solution, build from it a label for the problem, and then search for meaningful compliments. Therapists should not overestimate patients' awareness of and insight about what they do right. They are often so overwhelmed and painfully aware of what went wrong that they overlook or totally forget their strengths and successes.

The SST task may not be the full treatment of choice but rather a small step in the right direction. It is often useful to reserve more complicated and elaborate treatments (such as medications, systematic desensitization, self-hypnosis, or cognitive restructuring), for later sessions. The therapist's minimal intervention may prove sufficient, and it makes little sense to begin with an elaborate intervention before knowing whether the patient will stay for further treatment. For example, in Belinda's case, the therapist only asked her to take care of the sickly cat and left the decision of when and how to return to school up to her. Mrs. Jones enhanced the therapist's message and on the way out of the session handed Belinda the appointment slip, giving her the autonomy to decide about future treatment. Neither the mother, who had brought Belinda many times to doctors, nor the therapist thought that this would be the last session. Belinda did. First by deciding to go to school and later by deciding not to return to the second appointment, she clearly became her own healer. (The ways in which therapists empower their patients are explored further in the next chapter.)

Leaving an Open Door for Future Change

When concluding a potential single-session treatment, the therapist may ask whether the patient would like to make another appointment or would prefer to leave an open door to come back whenever necessary. If both the therapist and the patient conclude that one session is sufficient (at least for the time being), they can arrange for a brief follow-up phone call after an interval sufficient to allow changes to mature (three months is often an appropriate interval). It is important to avoid unnecessary feelings of separation anxiety or abandonment on either side. The therapist may add, "Please call me in one month to let me know how things have changed. If you don't call me, I'll be calling you in three months for a follow-up." An example is the end of the hypnotherapy session with Carla, who wanted to lose weight. When asked whether she wanted to make another appointment, she replied, "Let me first work on what I got from today's session." The therapist responded, "That's a good idea. I think after a hypnosis session, it is good to let things filter down and be absorbed. Call me after three or four weeks but no later than two or three months and let me know how things are going. In any case, I will call you three months from now, because I want to know how things change." Here, the therapist heightened the impact of the single session ("after a hypnosis session it is good to let things filter down and be absorbed") and then allowed the patient room to work at her own pace by providing a defined yet flexible time framework ("at the end of three or four weeks, but no later than two or three months").

In the case of Brian and his divorced mother, Brian thought that one session would be enough for the time being, but his mother was not so sure, since she was still frightened as a result of what had happened recently and needed to be convinced that Brian would not return to his old ways. This provided the therapist the opportunity to turn to Brian and say, "It seems to me you still need to convince your mom that the changes you have made in the last two weeks are for real and for good." An open-door policy was agreed upon.

Following Up

Calling to follow up on SST patients not only is a rewarding and learning experience for the therapist but often turns out to be a therapeutic event for the patients. Follow-up can help patients to consolidate their gains and own the responsibility for them, be reassured that their therapist cared enough to call them, and realize that not coming back to therapy does not necessarily mean that they are "bad patients." For example, Dorothy, Brian's mother, was called after a six-month interval and asked whether she had found the single session to be sufficient. She replied, "Yes, it was. We got home, and I thought to myself, will that be enough? But he started opening up to me like he never did before. I think what he got in his mind was that he would rather talk to me than to a stranger. Also, he knew I meant business." A follow-up also suggests to patients that SST is not necessarily a once-and-for-all deal. Indeed, a year after the session with Dorothy, she called the therapist after she had caught Brian late one night smoking "dope" with a friend. She was advised to let Brian know that if he continued to use any recreational drugs or alcohol, he would not be allowed to stay in the house (an approach that had proved effective a year earlier in response to the runaway and suicide threats). The therapist further suggested that if in the future she was concerned about Brian's drug use, the clinic could perform a complete drug screen. Nine months later, she called to request another family session. At that session, the therapist learned that Brian's mother had caught him in his first attempt to smoke and that there had been no further incidents. Dorothy was about to remarry and move to a new place, so the therapist met with them for two more sessions to discuss the transition from a single mother with a single child to a blended-family situation.

While this chapter has presented a short, simple, and effective road to successful SST, it is important to keep in mind that there are many alternative ways to approach such therapy. If one way does not work, you can always try another. Each therapist's individual approach, combined with the idiosyncrasies and therapeutic subtleties of each session, will make sessions richer, more complex, and therefore more challenging than the case studies presented in a book may appear. Though the cases presented here all had successful outcomes, they should not be considered as "scripts made in heaven."

This book advocates the need to learn, plan, and master different techniques for effective SST. As Zen masters (Suzuki, 1970) advise us, in order to reach "a beginner's mind," one first needs to gain mastery of techniques and inner confidence. Yet Bion's (1967, 1977) suggestion that the therapist enter each session "without desire, memory or understanding" so that each interaction has "no history and no future" is highly relevant to SST. Much of the power of SST lies in the "chemistry" of a first time, which gives the therapist an exciting opportunity for a fresh start.

Four

Empowering Your Patient

> When the patient recovers, the therapist should be able to say:
> "My treatment helped nature."
>
> *— Eric Berne (1966)*

Carla, the twenty-seven-year-old woman who wanted to lose weight with hypnotherapy (case discussed in Chapter Three), was treated in an effective SST focusing on her statement "I have always had the weight of being the ideal child" as a therapeutic pivot chord. When interviewed for a follow-up six months later, Carla had lost weight and kept it off. She reported having more energy and being more self-confident and focused with her life and career. She was very appreciative of the help she had received in the session, yet it was very clear that her decision and the natural process that followed it were what had made the change possible. She first made a decision (which was not discussed in the session at all) to go back to graduate school to get a master's degree so that she could improve her career options. She then realized that the only time in her life when she had been able to lose weight and keep it off was when she had gone away to college (which also was never mentioned in the session). Once she was back in school and looking for better job opportunities, she moved out of her mother's house. She stated that she realized that she was tired of attempting to please her mother and needed to become her own self. Being in school and supporting herself kept her more busy and focused. The main problem that she had brought into the session, being overweight, became a non-issue for her, and she described the weight loss as an effortless process.

Regardless of the therapist's competence, mastery of therapeutic techniques, or diagnostic tools, the power is in patients and the way they utilize the natural process of change. Most often, it is the patients who decide when to start and when to end treatment. Whatever therapists do or say, it is ultimately the patients who decide whether to use the prescription (or any other input) or ignore it. The various ways in which therapists can empower patients and allow the natural process of life to further support the therapeutic process are the essence of SST.

Message and Metamessage

The art of psychotherapy depends largely on therapists' ability to mobilize patients' resources to heal themselves. One of the central tasks of the first session is communicating to the patient the therapist's assessment and therapeutic plan in a way that will mobilize and intensify the patient's positive expectation toward recovery and change. The experienced therapist is likely to convey messages containing hope and autonomy for every patient. In keeping with this, it is important to be aware of the messages that the therapeutic plan itself may convey. For example, when a therapist suggests that a patient needs to check into the hospital to prevent the possibility of self-inflicted harm or plans a long treatment with several sessions every week because of long-term problems or signs of personality disorder, the patient may receive several unintended metamessages: (1) The therapist does not expect the patient to be able to take care of him- or herself; (2) the therapist (or the medical system) will take over the responsibility for the patient's life; (3) the patient is not likely to see results for quite some time.

Barbara, a forty-one-year-old woman who was seen in the SST project for feelings of despondency and unhappiness with her marriage, explained in the follow-up interview:

Over the years, I learned that time does take care of certain things. Otherwise, I try to solve it myself or at least figure it out. If that does not work, I go to therapy. I went to therapy several times in my life, and it tends to be analytical and long term. Before, when I decided to stop going, I would feel guilty, as if I were not a responsible or serious enough patient. Last time, I stopped going after three months because I felt better and was busy with other things. Now I know that I can use therapy very well even in one session and go on with my life on my own. It is interesting that at first (because of my previous perception of therapy), I was suspicious about what can be accomplished in one session. You know, when I finally reached out for help, I did not want to be dumped. I was concerned that the therapist would be more interested in his project than in me. In a way, when you seek help, you ask for some attention. I wanted to know that he cared and that I got sufficient attention. So I asked for some more hypnotherapy. He could not reach me by phone, so he wrote me a letter and went out of his way to give me a double session since I had to come from a very long distance. Quite frankly, I got a lot out of the first session and much less after that. I guess I just wanted to know that he cared. So if you see patients for one session, you want to make it very clear that they can come back as much as they want whenever they find it necessary.

One of the simplest yet most significant ways in which the SST therapist can empower patients is by giving them a congruent message and metamessage that they do have a choice and a real option to recover or change now and that the message "I believe in you and your ability" is not just words. What therapists can learn from Barbara's feedback is to be very available and very explicit about an "open-door" policy, which should be stressed at both the beginning and the end of the session. While therapists may fear that this will make patients more needy, the opposite is actually the case. Once patients trust that the door is indeed open, they do not have to use it so often. To summarize, the problem of the long-term therapist is how to bring about congruency between trying to empower patients (to help them to help themselves) and keeping them a long time in therapy. The problem of the SST therapist is how to maintain a balance between efficiency (bringing about therapeutic results as soon as possible) and empathy (with patients' needs and pain). An explicit and genuine open-door policy may help to provide that balance.

Factors Beyond the Therapist's Control

The single-session patients we followed up at Kaiser often described changes that had resulted from natural consequences of life events, such as moving to a new school or a new neighborhood, changing jobs, or forming new relationships with significant others. When the follow-up interviewer failed to ask patients what they remembered from the session, the therapists would sometimes attribute positive changes to indirect hypnotic suggestions or some other subtle therapeutic technique. But, on the whole, I realized that I had taken my interventions and my words much too seriously. Patients reported following suggestions that I could not remember having made. They created their own interpretations, which were sometimes quite different from what I recollected and sometimes more creative and suitable versions of my suggestions. In the psychotherapy research literature, such factors that bring about change are often referred to as "nonspecific factors." In his classic book *Persuasion and Healing,* Jerome D. Frank (1974) searched for the common features of all forms of psychotherapy and healing and concluded that "if therapy does produce some benefit, whether it is maintained or not, may depend primarily on factors that are beyond the control of the therapist. . . . The effect of succesful psychotherapy seems to be to accelerate or facilitate healing processes that would have gone on more slowly in its absence" (p. 334).

Every effective form of therapy uses natural processes of change with or without intention. When both intended and unintended processes occur simultaneously (which they usually do), it is hard to differentiate between them. Jay Haley (1987) tells about a patient he treated early in his career, a nineteen-year-old woman with uncontrollable intermittent shaking of her right hand.* The shaking had persisted through a year of therapy, and a number of neurological tests had proved negative. The patient was referred to Haley for treatment with hypnosis while her psychiatrist continued to work on the childhood roots of the symptom. Haley asked the young woman what would happen if her symptom became worse, and she said that she would lose her job, because she was having increasing difficulty even holding a pencil to write. Then he asked what would happen if she did lose her job, and she replied that her husband would have to go to work. She had recently married, and her husband was unable to decide whether to go to school or to go to work; in the meantime she was supporting him. This helped Haley to think of the symptom as the result of an interpersonal issue, a perspective that he was trying to use at the time. At first he felt that the problem could be viewed as a marital issue. However, further discussion revealed that the issue was a broader one. The patient's parents, who did not approve of the young man, had opposed the marriage and continued to do so. Her mother called her every day and asked whether she was coming home that day. When the patient pointed out that she was married and had her own apartment, her mother would say, "that will not last," and she continued to call, encouraging the young woman to give up her husband and return home. Haley concluded that the shaking right hand and the husband's behavior could not be explained without a family view. The husband seemed to feel that he could not please his wife's parents no matter what he did. If he went to work, he could not get a good enough job to meet their standards. If he went to school, his wife would have to work to support him. As a result of this conflict, he was incapacitated.

---

*This case is discussed in J. Haley, "Therapy — A New Phenomenon" in J. K. Zeig, (ed.), *The Evolution of Psychotherapy.* New York: Brunner/Mazel, 1987. Reprinted with permission from Brunner/Mazel, Inc.

Haley used a variety of skillful therapeutic interventions in this case, and the outcome was successful: The shaking hand was cured, the husband went to work, and the parents began to support the marriage. However, while congratulating himself on his success, Haley could not overlook another change that had occurred during the therapy: The young woman became pregnant. This meant that she would have to quit her job, and so her husband went to work to support her. Her parents did not want her back home with a baby, so they began to support the marriage. The symptom disappeared. Since the patient was in therapy at the time, therapy got the credit for the cure, and Haley got more referrals (Haley, 1987, pp. 19–20).

Pregnancy and birth are good examples of the powerful natural process of change that has a great potential for positive as well as negative outcomes. If this woman had not been treated at the time by two therapists, would she have been cured once she became pregnant? Haley thought that she would have been. I do, however, see a role for the therapist in such changes — not one isolated from natural events (so that it could prove itself scientific or effective), but one that helps the patients be free and open to use such events for their healing and growth.

Recently, I had the opportunity to interview the sister of an identified patient who had come for conjoint family therapy. What she remembered as therapeutic was not the session itself but the occasion of her father driving the family to the big city where the therapist's office was and having ice cream and fun together after the session — something that she did not remember ever having happened before, as her father had always been busy and unavailable for any family activities. The decision to seek help, the time taken off from work (or school) for the appointment, and, in the case of family therapy, the process of driving together to the hospital and waiting for the session are often mentioned as triggers for change.

When Pathology Prevails

Traditionally, therapists are expected in the first session to watch for signs of psychopathology and rule out the possibility of dangerous developments such as suicide, a psychotic process, and influences of psychoactive drugs. What does a therapist do when pathology prevails and the prognosis is poor? In the context of SST, the case study reported by the Tavistock group (Malan and others, 1975) is illuminating.* A single thirty-three-year-old woman complained of depression and suicidal ideation. Her history was one of severe traumas. She had been born in Poland and as an only child had been spoiled by her parents. When she was in her teens, the Germans had invaded Poland, and both her parents had been sent to a concentration camp. Her father had died there. Her mother had survived but returned in a chronically ill state, and six years prior to the session she had died. After the war, the patient became promiscuous and had a series of unsatisfactory relations with unsatisfactory men. She left school at the age of eighteen and drifted from one job to another, coping inadequately with all of them. After her mother's death, she had a breakdown; she neglected her flat, sold everything that was valuable, refused to work, and lived on money sent by relatives. Two years prior to the initial psychiatric consultation, she managed to escape to Britain, where she continued living in the same manner, drifting from one job to another, always feeling weak and exhausted, experiencing a variety of other physical symptoms, and having one unsatisfactory affair after another. After one of these miserable affairs, she became afraid of everything, cried all day, and felt that she could not carry on. It was that that brought her to the clinic.

The patient was diagnosed as having a depressive reaction in a passive-dependent, hysterical personality. One might argue that both her psychiatric and her life conditions were severe enough to call for long-term therapy. It might even have been appropriate to hospitalize her at first to reduce the risk of suicide. However, she was not offered treatment, because the psychiatrist felt that she lacked the motivation to help herself and the dis-

---

*This case is reported in D. Malan and others, "Psychodynamic Changes in Untreated Neurotic Patients, II. Apparently Genuine Improvements" in *Archives of General Psychiatry,* volume 32, 1975, pp. 110–122. Copyright 1975, American Medical Association.

cipline needed for psychoanalysis (which was the treatment offered in the clinic). No other contact with any therapist was made before or after that session.

As part of the research about "untreated patients," this patient was seen by a psychiatrist for a follow-up interview seven years after the single psychiatric assessment. He learned that shortly after the session she had begun to improve. She got a new job as a secretary. When she was fired from that job after five years, she immediately got another job as a secretary, which she kept thereafter. After a brief relationship with one man, she met and eventually married another and had been with him ever since. She acted in this relationship maturely and assertively. For example, when she first met this man, he was married to someone else, and she accepted his statement that he did not intend to marry her. When after two years of a very satisfying relationship she decided that she wanted to marry him, she was open and direct about it with him. After a few stormy months of "on again–off again," she told him that if he did not marry her, she would leave him. They parted for three weeks, and then he phoned her. She told him that she did not want to speak to him and was going to hang up, but he begged her not to do that and told her that he was going to start divorce proceedings. They got married seven months prior to the interview.

The patient described her husband and her marriage in very loving and glowing terms, yet she showed considerable insight when she said that she had been spoiled but had never been loved before. Although she described a very harmonious relationship, she gave evidence of being capable of empathy — for example, understanding why he was sometimes irritable — and handled it in an apparently mature way. All her symptoms entirely disappeared after the marriage.

This patient's single psychiatric consultation had focused on her traumatic and depressive history, and the psychiatrist offered no consolation, hope, or further treatment. The content of the session as well as the diagnosis and prognosis of the psychiatrist was grim. It would be hard to argue that any therapeutic interventions were tried here. Does her remarkable and unexpected progress in a course of seven years without any therapy suggest that she was not "really" depressed and did not have a "real" personality disorder? Can her changes be attributed to the fact that she had reached a point of no return and, when the psychiatrist offered her no treatment, finally decided to take charge of her life, realizing that there was nobody there to rescue her? Did she change in spite of all odds? Such unexpected and dramatic changes are susceptible to many more possible explanations as well as criticism (from a theoretical as well as a scientific point of view). Yet it is undeniable that a considerable number of patients are capable of recovering "against all odds" in ways that are very difficult to explain using plausible and logical thinking within traditional theories.

Empowering the Therapeutic Mechanisms

Most mental illnesses and human stresses can be seen as demands for change to which body and mind try to adapt. M. Scott Peck (1978), a great advocate of long-term therapy, writes in *The Road Less Traveled:* "We know very well why people become mentally ill. What we don't understand is why people survive the traumas of their lives as well as they do. We know exactly why certain people commit suicide. We don't know, within the ordinary concept of causality, why certain others don't commit suicide. All we can say is that there is a force, the mechanics of which we do not fully understand, that seems to operate routinely in most people to protect and to foster their mental health even under the most adverse conditions" (p. 238).

The Tavistock group (Malan and others, 1975) studied forty-four "untreated patients" who, like the patient described above, were seen for initial consultation but never received treatment. They concluded that untreated patients used nine different therapeutic mechanisms: (1) insight; (2) the capacity for self-analysis; (3) working through feelings with the people involved; (4) normal maturation and growth; (5) therapeutic relationships, especially marriage; (6) taking responsibility for their own lives; (7) breaking the vicious cycle between the patient and his or her environment; (8) genuine reassurance; and (9) direct learning. All of these mechanisms were used by patients who were not psychologically minded or therapy oriented (they dropped out after one consultation or were considered unsuitable for psychoanalysis). Yet these patients successfully employed what every long-term patient of psychoanalysis could hope for at the conclusion of many years of therapy. The lesson here is not that long-term therapy is useless but rather that one should never underestimate patients' capacity to change, including their capacity for long-lasting changes and psychodynamic insights, and should not overestimate the importance of therapy and therapist in reaching for those goals.

Kenneth Pelletier (1977, 1978), of the University of California, San Francisco Medical Center, studied patients who had recovered despite great odds and found five characteristics common to all of them:

1.   Profound intrapsychic change through meditation, prayer, or other spiritual practice. Such changes can be achieved via so-called scientific methods, such as psychoanalysis, hypnosis, and visualization, as well as so-called religious practices, such as Zen, yoga, transcendental meditation, and prayer. All use essentially similar mechanisms; the "right" choice is based on the patient's belief system and hopes.
2.   Profound interpersonal changes, placing the patient's relationships with others on a more solid footing. Apparently, people do not choose between intrapsychic and interpersonal solutions but employ both.
3.   Alterations in diet. These patients no longer took their food for granted. They chose it carefully for optimum nutrition. Once patients realize that healing is an active collaboration between the doctor and themselves, they can take an active role in determining which chemicals are consumed by their body.
4.   A deep sense of the spiritual as well as the material aspects of life.
5.   A feeling that their recovery was not a gift or spontaneous remission but rather a long, hard struggle that they had won for themselves.

The implication of these findings for SST is that each and every therapeutic encounter should convey the message (and the metamessage) that much of the recovery from pain and illness lies in mechanisms such as patients' ownership of their treatment and recovery and doctor's and patient's beliefs that they are part of a larger therapeutic system, including significant others, the natural environment, and some form of spiritual help. Patients with severe illness may recover against all odds and may have the inner knowledge of many therapeutic mechanisms without being in therapy or even being psychologically minded.

Waiting as Empowering

Realizing that the first session might be the last, what does the therapist do when his or her impression is that the patient suffers from character disorder, major depression, or any severe disorder that clearly requires more than one session? It might be useful to delay a decision about this for a little while. More often than not, the therapist will be surprised by spontaneous recovery in apparently difficult cases. For example, here is a conversation I had with a mother of a sixteen-year-old runaway and drug abuser whom I had seen in a single family session nine months earlier and who had not shown up for the adolescent recovery program to which I referred him:

Mother: It sure is hard to know what made him quit the drugs and the running away. My feeling is that by all of us coming in, we somehow were able to communicate to him that we really cared for him and we were not going to let it continue like that.

Therapist: Do you believe that was enough to bring a change to such long-term and destructive problems?

Mother: To tell you the truth, I did not believe this would be enough. Before coming in, I read quite a bit about the epidemic of runaways and drugs. I thought we were heading toward a long and painful shot. As a matter of fact, I kept insisting that we needed to come back to see you. My son kept replying, "Why don't you first give me a chance?"

Therapist: It sounds to me like he finally heard that you really cared for him and you were able to hear that he wanted to be given a chance to do it on his own.

Mother [laughing]:   I don't know if I heard him so well, since as a mother I continue to worry about a setback. But the reality of better relationships at home and no more horrors of the drug scene and running away convinced me to let go of him little by little.

In two cases with adult patients seen in our study, a patient with cocaine addiction was referred for treatment in a chemical dependency program and for a medical examination by a physician, while the other patient, with panic disorder, was referred for a combination of medication and group therapy. Follow-up interviews revealed that neither patient had followed the treatment plans; instead, both reported the fundamental impact of natural events (finding a job, falling in love, moving to a new place, the passage of time) on the clinical picture. Furthermore, even if it is clear to the therapist that the diagnosis is correct and the patient requires psychoactive medications, there is a very good chance that the patient either will not take the medications at all or will abuse them (for example, drinking alcohol while taking antidepressants). Good use of psychotropic medications and long-term treatment plans requires further commitment, resources, and motivated patients. The therapist may want to wait and see whether the patient builds up the required level of commitment and motivation to follow through with the therapist's agenda. Meanwhile, the therapist may use what has already been working, such as underlining the patient's existing strengths and available resources and prescribing solutions that are already within the patient's capabilities, belief system, and past attempted solutions.

If a therapist feels that without a particular treatment the patient will make no progress at all, it is recommended that the therapist carefully evaluate the likelihood of the patient's following through with his or her suggestion. Alexandra Levine, an oncologist from the University of California, Los Angeles, found that 60 percent of cancer patients treated on an outpatient basis who were prescribed chemotherapy medications later had no trace of medication in their blood samples (Siegel, 1986). If therapists want to prescribe, for example, antidepressants, they should find out first whether the patient believes in using pills or uses or abuses other drugs, as well as determining past performance with other doctors' orders. In other words, in the very first session, the therapist should try to minimize the chances that the main plan for treatment will be dismissed or abused. If there is doubt, the prescription should be saved for the next appointment, when more trust and ongoing working relationships can be built. Many failures in psychotherapy are a result of the right treatment being prescribed at the wrong time. If therapists prescribe what they know to be most helpful in a particular case but patients do not follow their advice, chances are that the therapists will view the prognosis as poor and will experience negative countertransference.

When a therapist feels that a patient's life will be in danger if the patient is not given the final diagnosis or treatment of choice right away, this is a clear indication for hospitalization (or else a sign that the therapist is playing omnipotent and underestimating the patient). When therapists decide to hospitalize psychiatric patients (especially if they are young adults and this is their first admission), they are not only determining that there is a risk of homicide or suicide (or other grave conditions); they are also setting in motion what often turns out to be a very long and disabling process of patienthood. Another rationale for the "hold your gun" approach is to avoid the set of expectations and self-fulfilling prophecies that often result from diagnosis of severe disorder. In following SST cases, therapists should allow as much room as possible for spontaneous recovery or self-correcting and random solutions to take their course. Mental health patients can be very vulnerable to developing dependency on their medication or therapist to an extent that they will attribute any positive change to the medication or the doctor. This is particularly common with the prescription of Xanax for panic disorder or Valium for anxiety and sleep disorder and with the prescription of long-term individual therapy for passive and dependent personality disorder. Patients in these cases are not only likely to attribute most of the positive changes to the power of the medication and/or the doctor but are also very likely to expect that symptoms will resume as soon as they go off the medication or terminate therapy. The notion of cure is at best problematic in mental health, and even a very conscious and competent therapist very often ends up providing open-ended therapy.

The approach suggested here might appear risky to therapists who wish to practice safe therapy with no legal risks. Yet being rushed by patients' anxieties or thinking of therapy from an attorney's point of view is rarely effective.

Empowering Patients with Opposing World Views

An important part of empowering patients is allowing their faith and belief systems to guide the healing process. At the same time, one of the most difficult obstacles to overcome in trying to empower patients is their following a line that the therapist strongly opposes or, worse yet, considers to be gravely wrong. The surgeon Bernard Siegel (1986) works with what he calls exceptional patients who sometimes, although they are terminally ill, refuse his advice to undergo surgery or receive medication and follow a strange passage of mystical healing and visual imagery of some ancient archetype. Siegel, a very unusual surgeon himself, eventually learned that these very "crazy" patients often have longer and better lives than their fellow cancer patients who follow doctors' orders faithfully.

When I first started to work with the concept of empowering patients, I often deceived myself into believing that I could always empower them by using my beliefs dressed up in their words. For example, because of my strong belief in the drive for health and the therapeutic value of positive thinking, I tended automatically to search for a metaphor and a relabeling that, by replacing words with negative connotations with words with positive ones, would shift the patient's thinking from viewing his or her condition as illness and pathology to seeing it as a challenge or even as a healthy sign. Sometimes this approach did not work, and the patient held to the negatives and kept talking about pain and pathological symptoms. Initially, I interpreted this as a sign that my intervention needed to be strengthened and intensified, and I tried harder to come up with a more powerful intervention in the same direction, fighting my patient's resistance in an uphill battle. Later, I realized that those patients needed to know that they had a very real illness and that it had a medical name before it would be possible to treat it. Once this need was satisfied, they were relieved, taking it as a sign that the problem was not "just in their minds" and that they were not "making it up." These patients would be very disappointed if I "normalized" their problem and would be greatly relieved when I gave them a diagnostic label and explained it in medical or scientific terms. For example, many of my alcholic patients are great believers in the Alcoholics Anonymous twelve-steps philosophy. Although I personally have many reservations about the disease concept of alcoholism, I have learned that some patients can heal by first accepting their problem as illness and that one can become powerful by first accepting one's helplessness. This idea was beautifully phrased by Jullie, a young woman who developed blindness as a result of diabetes: "Blindness taught me to see, and death taught me to live" (Siegel, 1986, p. 145).

When No Treatment Is the Best Treatment

Allen Frances and John Clarkin (1981) of the Department of Psychiatry at Cornell University Medical College studied 500 consecutive psychiatric evaluations and found that while in fewer than 1 percent of the cases (4 cases) the therapist had chosen no further treatment as the prescription of choice, more than 10 percent (52 cases) of the patients elected no treatment. They conclude that "The benefits of no treatment deserve more consideration than they generally receive. No treatment may serve to: (1) Protect the patient from iatrogenic harm (particularly to interrupt a sequence of destructive treatments); (2) Protect the patient (and clinician) from wasting time, effort and money; (3) Delay therapy until a more propitious time; (4) Protect and consolidate gains from previous treatment; (5) Provide the patient an opportunity to discover that he can do without treatment; and (6) Avoid a semblance of treatment when no effective treatment exists." (Frances and Clarkin, 1981, p. 545).

No treatment as the prescription of choice is particularly appropriate for patients who are likely to enjoy spontaneous improvement. The Finnish physiologist I. Kojo (1989) takes it one step further. He sees the placebo as a powerful tool in all medical treatments. He suggests that the placebo effect can be more general and long-lasting than effects caused by more specific agents and proposes that imagery is the intermediary between suggestion and the placebo effect. He concludes: "Thus placebo should be used intentionally together with treatments and drugs which have more direct physiological and pharmacological effects" (Kojo, 1989, p. 261). Yet, for therapists, it is most difficult to allow patients on their way to spontaneous improvement to recover without the therapist's input.

Very often when I present the results of our SST study or a case example to an audience, someone asks how I know that the change is the result of the therapist's intervention and not a spontaneous recovery, "flight to health," or some other variable. My answer is that I hope that these factors as well as others beyond my awareness did contribute to the patient's improvement. The factors that I labeled the natural process of change are every competent therapist's greatest allies. This was well recognized by Eric Berne: "A patient has a built-in drive to health, mental as well as physical. His mental development and emotional development have been obstructed, and the therapist has only to remove the obstructions for the patient to grow naturally in his own direction. The therapist does not cure anyone, he only treats him to the best of his ability, being careful not to injure, and waiting for nature to take its healing course" (Berne, 1966, p. 63).

The Natural Process of Change

We live in times of high technology with easy access to great amounts of information, which have resulted in a great body of knowledge and scientific breakthroughs. At such a time, we often overlook what we already have and what has always been there, the natural process of life and change: the turning of the seasons, sunrise and sunset, the moon's cycles, the wisdom of the plant, nature and human beings' maturation process from birth to death.

By using the term "the natural process of change," I try to emphasize the role of what is already there (natural), the healing role of time and movement (process), and the inevitable change that is already well under way when therapists first meet their patients rather than the notion of a steady state or being stuck at the same spot. There is an incredible therapeutic power hidden in these processes. When therapists combine it with the inner strength and knowledge of their patients, it can be utilized powerfully in even a single session of therapy. When each and every session is looked at in the larger context of its time and place, much more than you may expect can happen. If the existing natural processes (both internal and external) are tapped into, many changes will be noticed. If physical and human support beyond the patient, the therapist, and the therapist's office is utilized, much power and strength can be found.

There are many small and simple ways to reintroduce to the patient the potential power and health that lie in natural processes. Simple interventions such as taking a walk around the block for ten minutes, jogging for half an hour, swimming for an hour after work, or even spacing out and doing nothing about an overwhelming problem can be suggested in cases where there are what seem to be very severe and complex problems.

There is nothing new about those "placebo" interventions that allow nature to take its healing course. Ancient physicians were so familiar with the natural power of the organism to control disease that they invented for it a special expression, *vis medicatrix naturae:* "the healing power of nature." As Rene Dubos put it, "we cannot avoid being exposed to a multiplicity of physiochemical and biological agents of disease. We survive only because we are endowed with biological and psychological mechanisms that enable us to respond adaptively to an immense diversity of challenges. This adaptive response may be so effective that most challenges do not result in disease. If disease occurs, the adaptive response commonly brings about spontaneous recovery without the need of medical intervention" (Cousins, 1979, p. 15).

Simple Solutions to Complex Problems

The benefit of empowering the patient is not limited to reassurance of the worried well or prescribing minimal or no treatment to spontaneous recoverers. It can be equally important in severe cases with very real problems. A good example is Oliver Sacks's (1985) patient known as "the man who mistook his wife for a hat." The man suffered from a rare form of brain damage where his ability to abstract things was intact but his ability to recognize concrete items was severely damaged. As a result, he would make very funny mistakes, such as, when walking in the street, patting the tops of water hydrants or parking meters, taking them to be the heads of children, or, seeing a hat in his apartment, approaching it lovingly, thinking it was his wife. Yet these odd mistakes did not cause the patient much concern; he felt quite well and carried on his life as a distinguished musician quite successfully. Sacks, a renowned neurologist, was asked to examine this patient. After two days of extensive examination both at the patient's home and at the hospital, the patient turned to Sacks and said, "Well, Dr. Sacks, you find me an interesting case, I perceive. Can you tell me what you found wrong with me?" Sacks replied, "I cannot tell you what I find wrong, but I will say what I find right. You are a wonderful musician and music is your life. What I would prescribe in a case such as yours is a life which consists entirely of music. Music has been the center, now make it the whole of your life" (Sacks, 1985, p. 18). Sacks never saw this patient again, and it is very possible that medicine had very little to offer him. Therapeutically, I could not think of a better intervention in such a case.

Along with paying attention to the patient's special talents, the therapist should pay special attention to natural life cycles. For example, when treating a depressed patient, the therapist should find out whether the depression is affected by the change of seasons, whether sunlight might replace the need for medication or even cognitive therapy. With a terribly irritated and argumentative couple, the therapist might look for some tide or time cycles involved. Such cycles might be associated with the menstrual cycle, in which case the therapist might prescribe brief time-outs from one another or vitamin B_6 for the woman, instead of plunging into the dynamic of their relationship or teaching them how to fight more effectively.

Other natural processes are much more subtle, and it is only with the passage of time and trial and error that we can trace them. When I was in private practice doing mostly long-term therapy, I at one time accumulated a long waiting list. I felt bad about it, and when patients did not accept a referral elsewhere, I saw them for a brief evaluation of twenty minutes to decide whether the case could wait for a few months. At the end of the session, I would again tell the patients that I did not have any openings at that time but if they wanted to see me later, they could carry out various tasks and report back to me in three months, when I might have an opening. The tasks were always simple, such as reading a book that I thought would elicit self-help or awareness, daily physical exercises, or some interpersonal task with a significant other who might provide support or a healthy response. When these patients returned after three months with encouraging news of some spontaneous changes, I told them that I still did not have an opening and gave them another therapeutic task and a three-month follow-up. Seasons changed, time healed, and problems came and went.

Probing Empowerment

The concept of empowering the patient and tapping into the natural process might seem to some readers to be abstract or vague. Actually, utilizing this concept in SST is fairly simple. Various questions, statements, and therapeutic exercises can be used to elicit the power of the patient's knowledge, feeling, and behavior in the course of the first session. I first learned about this line of interviewing from Steve DeShazer and Insoo Berg by observing what they call "solution focused therapy." Below are some of the questions that might be used:

- "What would you like to accomplish today?"
- "What would you do/feel/think differently when you did not have to come here anymore?"
- "How would you know that you have indeed resolved this problem?"

- To patients who tend to feel that they are victims of others or external circumstances: "Let's imagine for a moment that you have 100 percent control over the situation. What would you do differently?"
- For patients who are badly trapped in their present situations: "Imagine that you are looking into a crystal ball and can see through it your situation two years from now. What do you see there?"
- For patients who are overwhelmed with a very big problem or multiple problems: "If you were to think of a very small yet significant first step in the right direction — nothing big, just enough to show you the light at the end of the tunnel — what would it be?"
- For "serious" or deeply depressed patients: "Now, I'm going to ask you a very difficult question, and I want you to think about it very hard. In those very few times that you were not depressed, what were you doing/feeling/thinking then."

When a patient who denies his or her own autonomy and power asks, "What do you think I should do/say about . . . ," the therapist can say something like "This is a very good/important/difficult question. Let me think about it and I will try to get back to it later today." Then the therapist can probe to elicit the patient's values, patterns, and previously attempted solutions regarding this subject. When therapists face truly unsolvable problems or ones that are beyond their capacity, they can say, "I do not believe I can teach you anything new, yet I wish to share with you some of the things I have learned from you today." The therapists can talk about what they experienced as the unique and genuine ways in which the patients struggled, often heroically and against all odds, with the problem, how they continued to love and care for significant others, how they did not give up on life, or what they have done that the therapist feels has eased the pain a bit. Nobody, including the most pathological and unfortunate patient, does everything wrong. The therapist may end such a session this way without advice, task, or directives.

The Therapist as the Underdog

When I was an undergraduate student in psychology, I took a course entitled "Change" taught by Ed Rosenberg. He asked the students to bring in personal accounts of events in their lives that had changed them in profound ways. In class, Rosenberg arranged for us to sit in a circle. He would listen very attentively to all the students' stories, usually with no interruption, and then would be silent for a few moments. He presented himself as a rather shy and insecure person, and I often observed his anguish and discomfort as he struggled with how to respond to the story told by one of us. He would close his eyes and toss and turn in his chair and finally begin to tell a story of his own. The stories were usually drawn from his childhood or youth or concerned one of his family members. They were often stories of struggle and pain, where the underdog (usually Rosenberg himself) was trying to find a way to grow and find a solution yet was always faced with a difficult dilemma: "Should I or shouldn't I?" He was a masterful storyteller, and many years later I still remember many of his stories. I do not remember him giving advice to any of us or even analyzing or making an editorial comment on our stories. The experience was for me like some kind of a Rogerian story or a Woody Allen movie where the hero is an antihero. Rosenberg placed his stories in a kind of a one-down position that always made me feel that I knew a lot more than I thought I knew and the knowledge was truly mine. At the conclusion of his stories, I often felt like giving him advice or walking across the room to hug and comfort him in his anguish. Of all the dozens of teachers I had in the course of eight years of studying psychology, I remember him the most.

Five

Single-Session Therapy in Action: A Case Example

> From one contact, a client may get some feeling of release from
> the pressure of a problem which has never been fully articulated
> but has been merely mulled over with frantic reiteration in his
> own mind.
>
> *— Elizabeth McCord (1931)*

This chapter presents the transcript of an actual session with an SST patient, somewhat condensed and edited to protect the patient's confidentiality. The interview was conducted three months after we started to experiment with planned single sessions. Some of what we know now (and is presented in Chapters Two and Three) we had not yet articulated then. In retrospect, we feel that the therapist could have done a few things differently. Yet this case had a satisfying outcome and provides a useful illustration of SST in action. While Chapter Four suggested ways in which the therapist can allow the patient and natural course of life to act as the powerful agents in psychotherapy, this case demonstrates how the therapist can be prudently active throughout the SST. Whereas therapists with a background in a very active form of therapy might want to learn more about being

Note: This chapter was written with Michael F. Hoyt.

"constructive minimalists" in SST, those who are more accustomed to acting mainly as "privileged listeners" in therapy may learn more from this case.

Starting the Session

The patient was a thirty-year-old Caucasian woman who had never been in therapy before. She had called our clinic a week before the session saying that she needed to learn how to deal better with her father, who was going to be released from jail soon. She needed to be ready for this event, because "I get all shaken up and fall apart when I have to deal with him." The therapist had allowed ninety minutes for the session; it lasted seventy-five minutes.

After the therapist had greeted the patient in the waiting room and introduced himself, he led her to the interview room. He asked her whether she would consent to the session being videotaped making it clear that she would receive the same treatment whether or not the session was videotaped and that she was free to decline. She reviewed the consent form and asked whether there would be any projectors or bright lights in the room. When she had been reassured about this, she said, "Sure, if it will help, yeah" and signed the consent form.

The therapist began the session by attempting to form a therapeutic alliance. In introducing himself and taking the patient's history, he emphasized change and a positive expectation that a helpful solution could be found.

Therapist: Well, as I said outside, I am Doctor Michael Hoyt. The purpose of our meeting today is to find out what problems you are having, what brings you here, and then to figure out what solutions would be helpful.

Patient: Yeah, that's what I need.

Therapist: Okay. Sometimes we can get everything solved in one visit. That is, if you are really motivated and want to get right down to figuring out what to do, we may be able to get everything dealt with today. If we are not able to, then we will figure out what the next steps are.

Patient: Okay. I am ready.

Therapist: Well, fill me in. What brings you here today? What's cooking?

Patient: Well, actually most of the problems started with my father. I grew up with a manic-depressive father, and we went through a lot of things as kids. I have three brothers, and my mom hung in there with us the whole time. He has been in and out throughout our lives. He was the best father when he did not drink, use illegal drugs, or get into a manic state. You know, he would be there for a while, and then his behavior would be rugged. He would try to twist our minds, brainwashing us. He would get all delirious and crazy. Then he would be in and out of hospitals and jails because he steals and lies. And then, when he got out, there were periods when things were pretty good betweeen my mom and dad. They split up and went back together so many times, trying to work it out and be a family. They finally divorced when I was in the sixth grade. Now I am married and have two kids, and my mother is happily remarried. My dad lives his own miserable life, and every now and then he will show up at my door.

Therapist: And what do you do then?

Patient: Recently, I had him staying with me from mid-January to late February. You know, I hear a knock at the door, I open the door, and there he is. Instinctively, I welcome him in, give him a big hug, and ask, "How are you doing?" and we sit and talk for twenty minutes. And yet this man frightens me to death. I am literally scared of him. He is the best of fathers one minute, and then snap, he has got a whole different personality. His mind is triggered in a whole different direction. That scares me.

Therapist: What are you scared is the worst that can happen?

Patient: You just do not know when it is going to come. When he gets manic it's like a constant brainwashing. It gets worse when I feel like he has got control of me somehow or some kind of power over me that can make me sit there and hear anything that he dishes out. He will not let go of the past. He just keeps throwing it up at us. All he does is dig up the past. I tried to erase it from my memory . . . I kept it all inside, but every time he is around or calls, it just gets all stirred up.

Therapist: So you have had to struggle with all of it practically all your life. Have you been in any psychotherapy or counseling before?

Patient: No. I just kind of kept tucking it away . . .

Therapist: So, it's finally gotten bad enough you are going to do something to get rid of this, you are ready to deal with it.

Patient: Yeah. I am ready. I do not want to go through any more of that. I do not want to have to deal with it any more. I do not want my kids exposed to it.

Notice how, early in the session, the therapist had already cultivated the patient's motivation ("you are ready to deal with it") and positive expectation ("figure out what solutions would be helpful," "do something to get rid of this").

Search for a Therapeutic Focus

By creating a therapeutic focus, the therapist can help the patient to feel less overwhelmed and confused. In choosing the therapeutic focus, it is often useful to go with what is presently most painful for the patient ("it has finally gotten bad enough," referring to the problem that impelled the patient to seek treatment). Yet the focus should have the seeds for a workable solution as well as an image or metaphor that can go beyond the presenting problem per se. Notice how in the next section the therapist repeatedly encourages the patient's sense of autonomy and self-determination while facilitating her description of her predicament and conflict.

Therapist: So, what is it that you would like to accomplish today?

Patient: I want to take it out of me, deal with it, and get it aside, and learn how to handle him when he calls, when he comes to my door.

Therapist: It sounds like there are two things you really want to accomplish. One is the stuff from the past that is eating away at you, you want to finally get it out and be done with it.

Patient: That is right. From childhood on he has dug it up. So now, I am flashing back, reliving a lot of it. It just keeps eating me away. I can't stop thinking about it. . . . And it just makes me a nervous wreck. I get into a whole emotional turmoil. He just makes me so mad, so torn up inside, I can't eat, I can't sleep, my stomach is in knots.

Therapist: So, that is one thing: dealing with your childhood. The second is how to deal with your father *now* when he starts to intrude into your life.

Patient: Yeah, I want to deal with it and learn how not to let him upset me. For years I just did not let him know where I lived, did not talk to him, and that worked. But he is not gone. He finds out where I live . . . I just wish he would never come around. Right now he is in jail. He called last night. I feel relieved [laughs nervously] because I know he is not going to be knocking at my door for a while. Isn't that terrible?

Therapist: No, it's really not terrible, given what you have been through. It sounds like you care about him. You do not want anything bad to happen to him. You just want him to back off.

Patient: Back off, that's fine. If he just wrote me letters. I could handle that, I think . . . but he keeps digging it up, constantly bad-mouthing and blaming my mother and my brothers.

Therapist: So which problem do you want to deal with first, the past or the present?

Patient: I do not know. I mean, I can't say one feels more important than the other. He still calls. He calls collect and tells me, "You are the only one who will talk to me. You are the only one." Last time he called, I blew up at him and said, "You know, ever since you were here and talked about Mom and the past, I am just torn up inside, my nerves are shot." He just said, "I am sorry, I am sorry," but he continues to do it. I do not know why I sat there and listened to it all, other than I have never given him a chance to speak his mind and say it all out. So I went through three days of listening.

Therapist: So he spoke his mind and said it all out?

Patient: Yes. And after he got through, that is when I knew that this has gotten to me. It was pretty bad. I went to take a shower and I literally wanted to jump out of the shower and run out and cry . . . oh, my God . . . I did not go. I just bent over and started deep breathing. I thought I would crawl out of my skin. I never felt all this before. I guess he just hit some point which tore me apart. He blames all of it on everybody but me, because I am the one opening the door . . . I let him come into my home.

Therapist: Opening the door for him, huh?

Patient: When we had him living with us, he was on his best behavior, because he knows my husband would just boot him out. But he let him stay, because, as I told my husband, he has to give me justified reasons to boot him out. I cannot just close, slam the door in his face . . . some days I say to myself: Yes. I can! It's when he makes me so mad, so torn up inside.

Therapist: So when you are mad enough you can slam the door in his face.

Working with the Metaphor

The patient has provided a rather concrete and useful metaphor that captures both the problem ("opening the door for him") and a possible solution ("when you are mad enough you can slam the door in his face"). The question now becomes what experience the patient needs to get unstuck from her emotional ambivalence and her position in the family as the only one who opens the door for her father. In the next section the therapist has the patient explicate the "rude things" her father has said and done to help her get unstuck by intensifying her revulsion. Notice that the therapist chose not to point out to

the patient how she victimized herself (accepting her father's collect calls, maintaining emotional dependency on her husband),
since she might use such feedback to feel more overwhelmed
or impotent. Instead, he acknowledged and validated her feelings and continued to elicit the part in her that knew what to
do. Often patients know what to do but lack the willpower and
clear vision to go after it. In the next segment, the therapist
uses empathic listening and paraphrases the patient's expressions to serve as a mirror for her presentation. Rehearing her
concerns, the patient is helped to gain more objectivity and
clarity about her problem.

Patient: This is what is so difficult for me. My brothers have
turned on him when he calls me. But I feel guilty as if I am
the only one left for him. There are no institutions for him. It
is just his own manic states that put him there. He knows the
game so well. So, as soon as he goes to a psychologist, he will
straighten out his act and get out. He has got them all fooled.
My dad has a way of brainwashing you. He can sit and talk
to you and you think he is just saying the nicest things, and
yet there is a twisted side behind it. And the next thing you know,
you are just shaking your head and going, "What?" You know
it's really twisted. I do not know whether that makes any sense.

Therapist: Sure.

Patient: I feel like I'm just talking in circles.

Therapist: Ahaa. The way you are talking about it is just the
way you experience it. It is hard to get a handle on this, so you
feel lost in it.

Patient: I do! I get lost in what he is saying. In how he says
that. He jumps from one subject to another and back to another.
And finally I got to the point where I said, "I do not want to
hear any more about the past. The past is the past and leave
the past alone." I dealt with him before in this manic state, living at my house. At that point, he was on his best behavior,
and he was there through right after we got married. One day
he came to the door with his head all gashed open and talking

delirious and saying rude things to me that a father would never say to his daughter.

Therapist: What kind of things? Crude things? Sexual things?

Patient: Yeah. Yeah. That I provoked him sexually as a child. Oh, my God, this is sick, he is sick.

Therapist: Did he ever come on to you when you were a kid?

Patient: No.

Therapist: Did he try to molest you or physically abuse you?

Patient: No.

Therapist: Good.

Patient: Yeah. I did not have to deal with any of that. Just when he threw that at me, I just thought how can a father talk to a daughter like this? I mean he cannot be in the right frame of mind, but that did not excuse it. It helped me to deal with it. And I told him: "You are sick. I do not want to deal with you. I do not want to talk to you. Stay away from me." That's what cut us off for five years.

Therapist: So you were able to cut him off for five years. So did other members of the family, like your brothers, who do not return his calls.

Practicing Solutions

The therapist now used the patient's language and experience and chose a concrete metaphor (slamming the door) to create a focus that could lead to a workable solution ("so when you get mad enough you can slam the door"). He underlined past successes and "exceptions to the rule" when the patient had drawn the line with her father ("So you were able to cut him off for five years"). From this point on, much of the therapy was designed to strengthen the patient's ability to follow through and overcome negative feelings (ambivalence, fear, guilt). Therapist and patient discussed various ways to stop the father's intrusion, with the therapist endeavoring to provide permission and encouragement. Notice how in the next segment the therapist uses the session to practice solutions experientially.

Patient: Well, I can cut him off from the calls, because he has to call collect.

Therapist: So you can just say, "I do not accept the call." The operator will tell him, "The party does not accept the call."

Patient: But when he sends me letters . . .

Therapist: You could write, "Return to the sender. Did not accept." Or you could tear it up and throw it in the garbage without even opening it. What do you think of that idea?

Patient: Sounds good. Doing it is just hard. Phone calls will be easiest. When he comes to the door, that is going to be rough.

Therapist: That is going to be the hard thing.

Patient: I remember being probably ten years old when we used to live next to my dad's sister. My dad and my brother went over to her house, and she opened the door, saw him, and closed the door in his face. Just like that. And I thought to myself: How could you do it? That is your brother at the door.

Therapist: So other people in this family know how to do it.

Patient: Yeah, but I used to think that was so wrong.

Therapist: That was when you were ten. Let's do an experiment, okay?

Patient: Okay!

Therapist: Now you are thirty. [Therapist directs the patient to the door of the interview room and stands behind her.] Now, open the door, look out, pretend he is there, imagine that you see him. There he is. He just knocked.

Patient: And he is going to start talking and walking in the door.

Therapist: So you need to stand in front of the door. How are you going to keep him out?

Patient: I will have to close the door. [Patient closes the door softly.]

Therapist: You did it.

Patient: Then, he is still going to be there.

Therapist: So open it again. Try it. Now, what would you say to him if he was standing right there?

Patient [a bit louder]:   I cannot talk to you. I do not want to see you any more. [Patient slams the door firmly. Patient and therapist return to their chairs.]

Therapist: All right! Let's talk about it. What are you thinking?

Patient: I could do it!

Therapist: You could!

Patient: I could.

Therapist: Of course you could. You said it and you did it. So how do you stop yourself? What goes on inside your head?

Patient: Guilt! There is my father standing at the door, and I am going to close the door in his face. I have grown up thinking how terrible that is, not even giving him a chance to talk or say anything.

Therapist: Of course you have given him a chance. You are thirty. You have given him a lot of chances. You have given him all you can.

Patient: Hurting him . . . I mean that is the bottom line. I know it would hurt him.

Therapist: You are a very loving, caring person. That is what makes it hard. If you were a cold-blooded person, you could do it with ease.

Patient: That is it! You know I got those cold feelings once after he said those [sexual] things to me. Then it was not hard. No man should ever say things like that to his daughter. I do not care what state of mind you are in. There is no excuse. And I told him, "You are sick. I do not want to talk to you" and hung up. No problem.

In the above segment, the therapist directs an experiential component to reinforce the desired change and to clarify resistances or barriers. He comments that the patient's belief that it was wrong to shut out her father "was when you were ten . . . . Now you are thirty." Note the somewhat concrete nature of the task. The patient says that she "can't just slam the door on him," so that becomes a literal as well as a symbolic metaphor for "drawing a line." The patient is encouraged to do, in a real way, just what she has contracted to do. The "talking cure" becomes the "doing cure"; plan becomes praxis. The therapist uses the patient's openness to the influence of an authoritative male to help her accomplish what she wants, rather than to exploit her as her father has done.

Strengthening

In the next segment, the therapist explores the patient's support for carrying out what she contracted to do. Notice how her ambivalence resurfaces and how the therapist acknowledges it while continuing to support her goal.

Therapist: What does your husband say?

Patient: You mean about my dad?

Therapist: Yes, and how you are dealing with him?

Patient: He says that I am just setting myself up to get hurt and that he has done me no good. He is right, and he does help me a lot. If it were not for him, I probably would not be here. He brings me back to earth. Gets my feet back on the ground. He is my support. Definitely.

Therapist: When he is there you are strong. If he were there, you would be okay.

Patient: Yes, if he is there, I would have no problem. But if he is not there . . . it is like my father has this power over me. Yet, he does not, he really does not, but for some reason in my head I . . . just instinctively, I react to him with open arms, when I would love to slam the door.

Therapist: You can have more than one instinct at the same time. You can have that feeling of wanting to greet him with open arms and also at the same time, you are still angry at him.

Patient: That's it. Hurt and anger. What am I going to get myself into if I let him in? When we were first married and he was living in our house and he got into that manic state and all the things that he said . . . [the patient goes on to describe how one night her father explicitly sexually propositioned her]. From that point on, I've had this claustrophobic feeling, that walls are closing in. I can't get in the back seat of a car, elevators, crowds, anything like that. This week, just before coming here, I was thinking about this, and it just clicked. I realized, it started right after he got crazy in my house. I can remember the first instance when I felt this anxiety or uneasiness. I got with my husband in the back seat of a friend's car, a small Volkswagen. I needed to get out so badly that I could have gone through the ceiling, it did not matter that it was made of steel.

Therapist: That was when your father was staying with you?

Patient: That was right after he had left and made some threats to my husband.

Therapist: Threats to your husband?

Patient: Yes. That if Tom, my husband, touches me, he was going to kill him.

Therapist: Touch you in what way?

Patient: He did not say. He just said, "If you touch my daughter, I am going to kill you." We left the house that night. We could not sleep there.

Therapist: Has your husband ever been physically mean to you or abusive?

Patient: In no way. Never.

Therapist: He did not mean touch you like slap you or hurt you? Did he mean touch you like caress you and kiss you, and like that?

Patient: I think it was a jealousy thing. I mean that is what I took it for. From that point on, I have had to deal with fear of airplanes and so on. It is getting worse and worse, and I wonder if any of this was triggered off by him, if the closing in is him . . .

Therapist: I think it is.

Patient: In my head I cannot get him out. The walls keep closing in around me.

Therapist: I think that you are right. The feeling of him closing in on you and you will be trapped or surrounded by him.

Patient: Yes. He is a trap. To me he is a trap.

Attempted Final Intervention

At this point, forty-five minutes into the session, the therapist (who is accustomed to fifty-minute sessions) decided to deliver his final feedback. He started by acknowledging the patient's ability to stand up to her father when he acted inappropriately.

Therapist: You know, I am impressed that you were able to draw a line. When he made sexual advances to you, you drew the line. You said: "That is disgusting. I will not put up with that at all."

Notice that although she drew the line only once (an exception to the rule), and that was five years ago (past success), the therapist underlines it in the present tense in an attempt to make the exception into the rule and to make it into a here-and-now reality. In the next segment, the therapist gives the patient his "diagnosis" in interpersonal and personal terms. He does not add a new task but instead consolidates what the patient has done constructively in the past and what was practiced and discussed in the session. Now he emphasizes her role and capacity for self-determination. To help her remember what she has learned, he asks her to put into words what she is "actually going to do when this meeting is over."

Therapist: There are two problems. One problem is your father. In reality, your father is bad news. He has threatened your husband's life. He has come on to you sexually. He's got all these problems and more. He is bad news. So one problem is how to protect yourself and your family from him. The second problem, which interferes with solving the first, is the guilt that you keep putting on yourself. Where you say, "Oh, but he is my father. I am his last one. I have to help him. Poor guy. I will hurt his feelings." You know what you need to do in order to stop him: the restraining order, the hanging up the phone on him, the slamming the door, keeping him away. But you keep stopping yourself because you think of things that make you guilty. You are defeating yourself with thoughts like "I am his daughter. He is hurting. I have to take care of him." When you stay clear on what you want to do and do not stop yourself, you can deal with him. It would be hard, but you can do it, and you have done it.

Patient: I have. You know I have.

Therapist: You can use one feeling to fight the other. There is one memory that makes you very angry, and when you get angry you are very strong and very clear. You have the memory of this obnoxious, terrible thing to say to a daughter. When you think about that, you are ready to slam doors, hang up, get rid of him. Then you are not guilty. You are angry! When you're angry, no one can mess around with you, can they?

Patient: No one! [Nods firmly in agreement.]

Therapist: So when you walk out in a few minutes, what are you going to say to yourself? What are you actually going to do when this meeting is over?

Patient: Draw a line. Draw a line!

Therapist: How and where are you going to draw the line?

Patient: I will start with the phone calls, because that is when I will hear from him next.

Therapist: And what are you going to do?

Patient: Not accept it!

Therapist: Perfect!

Last-Minute Issues

This could be seen as a natural place to end the session. However, it sometimes occurs that the dramatic nature of one problem keeps therapist and patient away from another problem that may be long-standing but less dramatic. In this case, the patient's claustrophobic reactions were overshadowed by the dramatic nature of the problems involving the patient's father and were brought up only in the last five minutes. As the therapist was closing the session and discussing a date for a follow-up, he paused and said:

Therapist: Before we stop today, is there anything I have not asked or you have not said that you think is important to mention now? Or that you wanted to ask?

Patient: How do I deal with this claustrophobic feeling I have? I hate it. My husband hates it. There are many times when it has created a problem. Just today, I got panicked taking the kids in the elevator up to the dentist.

The therapist would be justified in saying at this point, "Our time is up. Why don't you bring it up first thing in our next session, and we will discuss it then." It might even be argued that such an approach would be therapeutic, since the therapist is trying to help the patient to "draw the line." And this could model setting limits. In addition, it is generally not a good idea to address a separate problem in the same session after successfully completing a piece of work, since this may result in losing the thrust and clarity of the former without achieving much success with the latter problem. "Quit while you're ahead" is usually good advice. (As discussed in Chapter Three, it would have been preferable to inquire about last-minute issues before attempting to conclude the session, rather than as an afterthought.)

In this case, however, being part of a study, the therapist decided to pick up on this last-minute issue, hoping to capitalize on the momentum that had been created. Extra time was available, and the therapist thought it possible that the patient's "additional symptom" could be resolved within the focus that had already been created.

Therapist: When did it start?

Patient: This started a way back, right after I had this terrible encounter with my father. Over the years, it's gotten worse. I used to love to fly. And now I get scared as soon as I have to walk down that ramp. It's my own mind. The more I think about it, the worse it gets.

Therapist: Until that encounter, when your father was outrageous and you got angry, before that, did you ever have any claustrophobia? Was it okay to be in little places, in back seats, small rooms, and all that? You would not get uptight?

Patient: No. I would not give it a second thought.

Therapist: So it all started after that time.

Patient: How does it start . . . claustrophobia, I guess you would call it. I mean the walls caving on me and I cannot breathe. Is that just something that builds up in your mind and then gets larger if you let it?

Therapist: Yes. That is a good way to describe it. It starts in your mind. You can kind of just worry about it. How am I going to do? You start to get panicky, and you worry: "Ha, I'm getting so tense." And you can kind of scare yourself, and then it snowballs. Sometimes it gets started when somebody feels themselves in a situation where they feel really trapped. Sometimes it's because they are physically trapped, like they get trapped in an elevator. Other times it is when they get trapped the way you felt trapped with your father. It is more psychological. You felt like you were trapped by him. Here he was coming on to you. One thing that is going to help this situation is if you really keep reminding yourself and keep drawing the line. Remind yourself that you are back in control instead of him controlling you and him trapping you. If you can say things like "I am back in control. I am angry. I made up my mind. I will not take this anymore. I am in control." So the walls are not caving in anymore. The second thing that is going to help is when I call you in a month (or when you call me), I will ask you how things have changed, and you will be able meanwhile to do some practicing. What you need to do is every day, little by little, try going into situations where you are slightly uncomfortable. Just slightly uncomfortable. And then stand there until you relax. So that you can let go and face the fears. Just stand there and breathe for a few minutes and get yourself relaxed. And then say that's enough for today, and then you can do it a second time. And then the next day you can stand on the first stair, notice that it's a little cramped, that is okay. And then you might go out to the car and just look in the back seat, the one that's got a small enclosed space. Do that for a day or so and relax. Then say to yourself, "Hey, I am in control, I am okay." and then for a day or two, with no one else in the car, go sit in the back seat for five minutes until you can get yourself relaxed. Just gradually put yourself in just slightly more confined places. Now, I am not saying to go tomorrow and get yourself buried alive in a space capsule or something like that, you know.

Patient [laughs]:   I know what you mean.

In the next few minutes, therapist and patient explored various locations to practice the relaxation and gradually confront her fears. Then she said:

Patient: It makes me feel better already. It is like the light at the end of the tunnel [laughs]. I hate tunnels too. I just stop the car. I cannot get myself in there.

Therapist: The light is coming, and it's getting bigger.

Patient: Oh, I like that. As long as I see the light.

Therapist: You can also lighten the load you have got by taking control and not letting him run your life anymore. So you're not trapped.

Patient: Exactly.

Therapist: Good.

Patient: Be in control and not get trapped.

Therapist: All right. Let's speak in a month. Let's speak on the phone. Give me a call. If something comes up before and it is a question that can wait, wait. But if it is something that you have got to know or have to ask something, do not hesitate to call me.

Patient: Like if he comes up with a new trick.

Therapist: You have got tricks too. You can fight back.

Patient: Yeah. Now that I know how!

Therapist: Yes! [shakes patient's hands firmly].

The therapist used the momentum of the session and tied the main theme of the session (drawing a line to regain control) to the phobic symptoms. The patient had revealed earlier in the session that the symptoms had begun after her father had invaded her home and sexually propositioned her, and this allowed for the interpretation that her claustrophobia was a manifestation of feeling her father "closing in" and "surrounding" her. She agreed: "He is a trap." The therapist used a combination of techniques (behavioral desensitization, cognitive affirmation, hypnotic suggestion) to help her feel "untrapped."

Follow-up: Outcome

The follow-up interview was conducted six months after the session by a different member of the study team, who knew only of the presenting problem as stated by the patient in the initial phone call:

Interviewer: How are you doing now?

Patient: I feel much better as a result of being able to confront my father and be clear with him. Things have improved a lot. Talking with Dr. Hoyt, I realized how irrational it was to let my father go so far. Now I am also generally not as shook up and paranoid as I was before the session.

Interviewer: What do you remember from the session?

Patient: I remember everything.

Interviewer: What do you recall that was particularly helpful or harmful?

Patient: It was helpful in talking it out, realizing the guilt feelings and that I don't have to take it anymore. I felt relieved in a big way. I am very satisfied.

Interviewer: Was the one session enough for you?

Patient: Yes. Since that session, I confronted my father and drew a clear line with him. He has not tried to bother me since.

Six

Learning from Failures

Failure is an opportunity for learning, a vehicle for becoming better therapists.

—Jeffrey Kottler and Diane Blau (1989)

An important lesson can be learned from each and every failure. In the literature to date, most assessments of the success or failure of SST have been based on the clinical notes and diagnosis of the treating therapist. When patients reject therapists and therapy after one session, they are not likely to leave without some harsh words being recorded in the therapists' report. In this book, the success or failure of SST is judged by patients' retrospective self-reports. Failure is defined here as cases where (1) patients reported no progress or worsening of the presenting problems, (2) patients perceived, in retrospect, the SST as insufficient, or (3) patients were not satisfied with the outcome of the single session.

In the sample of fifty-eight cases that we followed up at Kaiser, ten patients reported no change in the presenting problems, and one reported that the problems had got somewhat worse. Only four of these eleven patients had been seen for only a single session. The other seven had been offered and received more therapy after the initial session and before the follow-up.

Four (13 percent) of the thirty-three patients who were seen only once thought in retrospect that SST had not been sufficient. With the patients in this sample, the therapists attempted to reach mutual agreement to SST as often as possible; the percentage of failures is likely to be higher when SST is not anticipated or planned by the therapist. In many psychological studies and clinical practices (DuBrin and Zastowny, 1988; Baekeland and Lundwall, 1975), all single-session patients are automatically considered failures, since they are seen as cases of patients dropping out of treatment prematurely. However, dropping out simply means that the patient ended treatment earlier than the therapist perceived as appropriate. The cutoff point for considering a patient to be a dropout may vary. Levinson and others (1978), investigating a psychoanalytically oriented private-practice population, considered all patients who stayed in therapy eight months or less to be dropouts. Those who agree with this perspective are likely to conclude, with DuBrin and Zastowny (1988, p. 393), that "A substantial number of clients will drop out of treatment before they are able to complete a therapeutic process, resolve presenting complaints and achieve their goals. This will happen sometimes unpredictably preempting the opportunity for effective intervention. Rarely in these cases is it known what actually happened. Frequently in cases of client-directed and 'premature' termination therapists are left feeling bewildered, rejected, and angry, while 'labeling' themselves or, more often, their clients as failures." For those who are devoted to long-term private practice and want to avoid this kind of failure, the best bet would be to limit their practice to white, upper-middle-class educated and motivated patients who have already made a decision to commit a sizable amount of time and money to their treatment. By the time they arrive for their first session, such patients will already have searched for the "right" therapist and made their choice. DuBrin and Zastowny studied 426 patients primarily from such a population seeking long-term treatment therapy in group private practice in upstate New York. Only 57 patients (13 percent) failed to return after the first session. In a practice that includes patients from lower socioeconomic classes, minority-group patients, patients with less than a college education, and those with severe psychopathology, the chances of avoiding a large number of single-session encounters are very slim (Dodd, 1971; Bergin and Garfield, 1971; Lorion, 1974; Garfield and Bergin, 1978).

Dropouts can be seen as the result of a failure in communication between the therapist and the patient in attempting to reach a mutually agreed-on contract about how and how soon they anticipate the problem to be resolved. There is a clear discrepancy between what most therapists see as an appropriate length of therapy (often described as a matter of years) and the average length of therapy in reality (from four to six sessions). Furthermore, not many therapists negotiate the expected length of treatment with their patients. They often view therapy as an open-ended process. When patients dare to ask how long the therapy will last, therapists rarely commit themselves to the expected length of therapy unless such a limit is enforced by a third party (for example, an HMO, EAP, or insurance company).

The remainder of this chapter presents some examples of SST failures and the lessons that can be learned from them.

When the Therapist Terminates Too Soon

Joan called requesting therapy for Shelley, her seven-year-old daughter from a previous marriage. A week earlier her husband, Terry, had physically assaulted her while he was drunk, and the daughter had witnessed it. Immediately after the incident, Joan and Shelly went to a woman's shelter, where Joan was advised to call the clinic for an assessment of her daughter's reaction to the violence. A couple of days before the SST, mother and daughter returned home. Shelly was scheduled to leave town soon after the session to spend the summer with her biological father in Palm Springs. Joan, Terry, and Shelly attended the first session. The couple entered the session holding hands, and it seemed that the violence and the brief separation had led to a kind of second honeymoon for them. Joan and Terry were affectionate and supportive of each other throughout the session. Terry's drinking was assessed and discouraged, ways to maintain sobriety and prevent relapse, including AA and the clinic's chemical dependency program, were discussed, and alternative ways to resolve conflicts and break violent cycles were explored and experimented with in "as if" scenarios. The therapist observed Shelly's reactions and asked her to draw her family, her pets, and their house. In the second part of the session, the therapist inquired about the stresses of the couple's first year of marriage, when they had started a new business together and tried to blend his son from a previous marriage and her daughter into a new family.

Toward the end of the session, Joan suggested that Shelly might feel freer to talk one to one with the therapist. The therapist readily agreed and spent fifteen minutes alone with Shelly. She was responsive and warmed up quickly toward him. They discussed her drawing, her favorite games, and her memories of her stepfather's attack on her mother. Nothing in her verbal or nonverbal behavior or her drawing indicated pathology or an adjustment disorder. Joan and Terry were invited back to the room, and the therapist shared his observations with Joan, providing reassurance. Terry and Joan were given a task for further building up their courtship before Shelly returned from her summer vacation with her father. Finally, the therapist suggested that Joan call to schedule a follow-up as soon as Shelly returned. She did not call.

In a follow-up interview four months after the SST, Joan reported that there was no more violence and that they were doing better as a family. Yet when asked how Shelly was doing, she reported that since the incident Shelly had been very edgy and nervous, and small arguments bothered her a lot. When Joan and Terry raised their voices at home, Shelly got very upset. When asked how people around her had seen Shelly change, Joan replied, "I am the only one who sees a problem. At school she is doing fine. Last week I got a special note from her teacher saying what a good attitude she has at school. Our friends recently commented how nice she turned out to be." Yet it was clear that Joan's agenda had not been met. She concluded, "She needs to see somebody to talk to, somebody other than myself or Terry. Somebody outside of the family. I do not know how to get her to express her feelings. He [the therapist] talked to her alone for a few minutes, and it does not seem possible to do that much in one session." This feedback made it clear that Joan had felt a need for longer therapy than SST and for individual instead of family therapy. This failure in communication stemmed from various factors:

1. The therapist, who was part of a research team on SST and oriented toward family therapy, failed to notice the mother's preference for individual and longer therapy and proceeded without asking her at the beginning of the session how and how soon she hoped to solve the problem.
2. The mother requested that the daughter be seen alone only a few minutes before the end of the session.
3. The therapist did not schedule a second appointment, yet he did not present the therapy as SST but rather left it up to the mother to schedule another appointment. A battered woman can have difficulties asserting herself (especially with a male authority), and the therapist overlooked this possibility.
4. The therapy focused on what the therapist defined as the presented problems (the husband's drinking and violence and the blended family in transition) but failed to address the mother's problem ("I do not know how to get her to express her feelings"; "she needs to . . . talk to . . . somebody outside of the family"). As long as the complainant perceives a problem, there is one.

When the Therapist Intervenes Prematurely

As discussed in Chapter Three, the effectiveness of SST is determined largely by the therapist's ability to evaluate not only whether the planned intervention is correct but also whether the timing (readiness, maturation) is right. A case of the right intervention at the wrong time is that of Fran, a twenty-five-year-old woman who sought therapy after a boyfriend, who tended to drink too much and then become abusive toward her, moved in with her. In describing the problem, she said, "I told him to leave, but he refused. I am scared of him. What should

I do?" The therapist chose a very direct and authoritative approach to get the boyfriend out, suggesting measures such as obtaining a restraining order and calling the police.

At the follow-up, Fran reported that the boyfriend had moved out and the relationship had terminated. Yet she felt ambivalent about the results. She had left the boyfriend an open door to come back and felt lonely staying by herself. "I don't know if I did the right thing. Better if I had stretched myself more and let him stay." She acknowledged that things were somewhat improved: "I like having my space back, doing more of what I want to do. I don't have to endure his drinking and bouts of violence." She was mildly satisfied with the session and acknowledged that the therapist made her feel that she had "more control and could do something." One might argue that when domestic violence occurs, no timing is wrong for immediate action. Yet this woman was still in a position to invite further abuse from the same man. She could have benefited from some smaller steps in the right direction, such as joining a self-help group of "women who love too much," visiting a women's shelter, talking to women who lived with violent spouses, taking a course in assertiveness training, or possibly engaging in a longer treatment to gain more insight about her mate selection and her pattern of interaction with men.

When the Patient Feels Abandoned by the Therapist

One of the main risks of SST is leaving the patient feeling abandoned. Insecure, passive-dependent patients might be all too eager to please the therapist, reporting progress or satisfaction while seeking the therapist's attention or love. Jody, a thirty-seven-year-old woman, arrived to a session without clear symptoms or problems. She had recently been seen by a private psychotherapist, but that relationship had been terminated because of the therapist's illness. Jody was single and was to a great extent emotionally and financially dependent on her parents. In the session, Jody appeared somewhat depressed and anxious. Her speech was a little tense with very tangential, ruminative, and obsessional thinking. The therapist found it hard to get a focus or a comfortable flow to the session. (Jody reported in follow-up feeling interrupted by the therapist. When asked about her job, Jody said that she resented it and claimed to have many conflicts, hassles, and harassments. She had been working for a long time on becoming a poet, but her obsessive tendencies kept her from submitting her work for publication. Toward the end of the session, the therapist did hypnotherapy using the crystal-ball technique to improve Jody's creativity and ability to reach an independent decision. Because of the lack of focus and the patient's personality (dependent, obsessive, with border-line tendencies), the therapist did not find her to be a good candidate for SST. He gave her an assignment to complete a creative task that she was currently working on and asked her to return for a second appointment as soon as her work had been completed and submitted for publication. Jody was referred to a psychiatrist for the possible use of medication.

A few weeks after the session, the therapist received a very exciting letter from Jody, detailing some very positive and significant changes in her life and including her completed poetry, which she had submitted for publication. She did not request a second session. The therapist took the letter as a message that Jody was doing fine on her own and did not take any action. When called for a follow-up, Jody reported that she was not satisfied. She said that she had wanted more than one visit and felt abandoned by the therapist. She had not followed up with the suggestion to consult a psychiatrist and had not seen another therapist. Jody indicated that the positive changes were still holding on and that, among other things, she had got a new job (with higher pay and better atmosphere) and made a new male friend.

In reviewing Jody's case, the therapist wrote, "She loved the session and had made changes at the follow-up, but was enraged at not being seen more (and perhaps not having her poetry appreciated more!)." It turned out that Jody's father was a psychiatrist, and it was possible that what Jody hoped would result from her letter was that the therapist would congratulate her for being "a good girl who turned in her homework" and ask her to come back. She was offered further therapy but did not gain much more from it, although it revealed a clearer clinical picture of a borderline personality disorder.

The following lessons can be learned from Jody's case.

1. When many issues of independence and separation are un-
    resolved, the patient is unlikely to perceive SST as sufficient.
2. When the patient is unable to become targeted in the ses-
    sion and has multiple and vague complaints, more therapy
    is indicated.
3. When the therapist is unable to reach clarity about the case
    or feels that the patient should be seen by another profes-
    sional, some form of treatment should be continued. In
    Jody's case, it seems that the patient's dependency needs
    and obsessive qualities "got on the therapist's nerves" and
    that he was too eager to terminate and too quick to take
    her letter as an indication for a mutually agreed termination.
4. When the therapist gives a patient a task and wishes to make
    the next session conditioned on completion of that task, it
    is wise to set a timetable, with a scheduled follow-up ap-
    pointment. The therapist can ask the patient to call if the
    task is not completed on schedule so that the next session
    can be rescheduled after it has been completed.

Patients suffering from severe psychopathology, particularly borderlines, manics, and schizophrenics, present a difficult
challenge to the SST therapist. The therapist will be inclined
to offer them further appointments (since they are clearly needed), yet they will often fail to reappear and so become SST cases
anyway. In such cases, it might be useful to spend more time
in the first session evaluating their past therapeutic encounters
and developing a better prognosis. Patients who have long
histories of being "negative responders" or "nonresponders" to
psychotherapy might actually be good candidates for SST. The
therapist can be frank with them, saying that what the therapist has to offer is not likely to help them and suggesting possible alternatives (medications, halfway houses, self-help support
groups). If the prognosis is guarded or the patient is gravely
disabled, the therapist should be prepared to follow up after no-
shows (there will be more than one). With or without psychotherapy, this kind of patient requires routine follow-ups for a
few years in order to establish any reliable outcome.

When the Patient Rejects the Therapist

When patients come to "shop for the right therapist," it is best to focus the session on their expectations of the therapist and therapy rather than starting therapy right away. In such cases, if therapists focus on the presenting problem, they are likely to fail.

Ron, a thirty-nine-year-old man, felt depressed after a recent separation from his wife. The therapist suggested that Ron join other recently separated people in group therapy held at the clinic and added that Ron might need to accept the fact that his marriage was over. In the follow-up four months later, the patient reported that he and his wife were back together, but the problems were the same as before, and so was his depression. He had not joined the group but had gone to another therapist, whom he had seen weekly for the past three months. "I was looking for a Rogerian therapist and I found one," he explained. When asked how he had found out what kind of therapy he needed, he revealed that he had been shopping for a therapist for quite some time, had taken undergraduate studies in psychology, and had seen four therapists before coming to this clinic. He was unable to specify how any of the other therapies had helped him. About the single session he said, "I do not believe much can be solved in one session. The therapist's suggestion that my marriage might be over was a little off the wall and not the right message for me at that time."

There are several lessons to be learned from this case. First, although the history of previous therapy was a standard question on the clinic's intake form, the therapist failed to pay attention to this issue. With "experienced" patients, the therapist should find out early in the first session what they have got out of therapy so far and what their expectations are this time around. Second, the therapist should always find out how and how soon the patient expects to be helped. When a patient looks for a therapist to be an empathic and understanding listener, it would be better not to gear that patient toward change, certainly not in the first session. The need to be heard, understood, and cared for is a legitimate issue in therapy. Third, the therapist failed to check the patient's readiness for the divorce and the extent of the finality of that event. The therapist assumed that since the patient was separated, he needed support in accepting that state. However, recently separated people may seek therapy in order to reconcile their marriages, just as people may seek marriage therapy in order to justify their wish to divorce (the hidden agenda may be to satisfy their conscience or their spouse that they have done everything possible to save the marriage). Finally, the therapist should not become so concerned with the precipitating event (in this case, the recent separation) that other issues might be overlooked. By focusing prematurely on helping the patient in his divorce process, the therapist failed to realize that the patient was actually shopping for a therapist who would understand him without demanding any change, and so he responded negatively to the therapist's intervention.

Similar problems exist with uncommitted patients. When patients are referred to therapy by a third party (court, school, employer) or are in therapy in order to meet the needs of someone else (such as their parents), therapists may want to devote more time to two questions: (1) What is the patient's hidden agenda (often hidden from the therapist but known to the patient) in coming to see the therapist now? (2) Is there a problem (perhaps a different one from the presenting problem) that can be targeted and that the patient is motivated to resolve? For example, "What needs to be done to get your parents (employer, police, or other authorities) off your back?" might capture such a patient's ear better than figuring out "why using drugs is destructive" or "what you need to do in order to get off drugs."

When a Few More Sessions Are Necessary

The potential power of the first therapeutic encounter is undeniable. Often, much of what is done in the following sessions is derived from that first session and aimed at strengthening its results and conclusions. In 41 percent of the sixty consecutive intakes in planned SST studied at Kaiser, the therapist and the patient readily agreed that more than one session was needed, and the same therapist continued treatment until therapy was terminated. Those cases were followed up in the same manner as the SST cases. The researchers had anticipated that in those cases either the treatment would be diagnostically and therapeutically more difficult than the SST cases or in follow-up the patients would indicate more improvements and more satisfaction as the result of more sessions. However, results showed no significant differences between SST and non-SST cases in ratings of improvement, satisfaction, or ripple-effect changes. Furthermore, qualitative analysis of the two groups did not reveal significant differences in the level of difficulty of the presenting problem or *DSM-III-R* diagnosis. The lack of correlation between the severity of the problem and the length of treatment also appears in other reports of psychotherapy practice (Knesper, Pagnucco, and Wheeler, 1985; Knesper, Belcher, and Cross, 1987). When some correlation is found, it is often negative—that is, the young, verbal, functional, and affluent receive much longer therapy than the dysfunctional, old, and poor, and the longer the treatment, the lower the benefit. The following case example illustrates some of these issues.

Linda, an attractive woman in her early thirties, came for therapy along with Ricky, her sixteen-year-old son from a previous marriage. Ricky had become upset when his mother and John, his stepfather, got into a physical fight and had come to his mother's rescue by hitting John on the head with a baseball bat. John had left the house barefoot and bleeding, called the police, and gone to an emergency room, where thirty stitches were required to stop the bleeding. Linda, who was shaken by the whole experience, had called our clinic, and the family was seen the following week. Although invited, John did not show up for the first session. Linda said that it was she who had started the fight. She reported being irritated and aggressive as a result of premenstrual syndrome (PMS). That day, she had tried to engage her husband in an argument and, when he did not reply, had yelled and attacked him physically. John retaliated but was frightened by his own reaction and left the room, heading outside. Ricky, who heard the fight in his room, grabbed the bat, opened his door, and saw John leaving the master bedroom. He assumed that it was his mother who had been attacked and proceeded to hit John. Ricky readily admitted that he did not respect his stepfather and resented his attempts to discipline him. Linda had been a teenager when she became pregnant with Ricky and had been physically abused by Ricky's father, whom Ricky had not seen in eight years. In the session, Ricky admitted to being very worried about his mother when she got "crazy" and violent during bouts with her PMS.

During a consultation break near the end of the interview, the treatment team noted the many tensions and twisted alliances in the family as well as the various individual psychological problems and Linda's possible hormonal imbalance. The dramatic nature of the family violence stimulated the team to come up with several clever strategic interventions. One was to prescribe a family trip in which the family members would have to be cooperative in order to succeed. Another was to learn a new war game in which their conflicts could find a more symbolic expression and they would have to exercise restraint and negotiate à la the Geneva Convention. These ideas, as well as psychodynamic interpretations of the family members' individual motives, were discussed, but the ideas were not used. Instead, the mother was referred for consultation with a gynecologist and given a reference to a book about PMS. She was also told how to invite her husband to the next session so that he would feel included and an important contributor to a better solution. Ricky was complimented for caring for his mother but also reminded that he was neglecting his own extracurricular interests. Considering the dramatic nature of the problem, the absence of John from the session, and the need for medical evaluation, the treatment team agreed that longer therapy was indicated.

At the second session, all three family members attended. They reported marked improvement, and the session was devoted to underlining and strengthening the changes toward better-defined family boundaries and hierarchy. The therapist used structural maneuvers (Minuchin and Fishman, 1981) to direct those changes. In the third session, the family reported improvement in Ricky's school performance and relationship with John, and John announced that he had decided to formally adopt his stepson. The therapist expressed concern that the situation seemed too good to be true, so that there might be the possibility of a relapse, and devoted much of the session to different relapse scenarios using "let's pretend" family games as described by Cloe Madanes (1981). A few days before the fourth session, the mother called asking to terminate therapy since things were working fine and she felt that her last PMS period had been "much more under control." The therapist suggested that she call again a month later to report how the next PMS period went and added that in any case one member of the treatment team would call to follow up three months later. Below is a part of the follow-up interview.

Mother: Things have much improved in our family. It is going really well, and we handle a lot of things differently. Once in a while, communication becomes a problem, but it is a lot better than it was when we first came in.

Interviewer: What things made the change possible?

Mother: Talking about it in the open and seeing through somebody else's eyes. The suggestions were helpful, especially because we all wanted to work hard and make things different.

Interviewer: Besides the specific issue of violent fights, have there been other areas that have changed?

Mother: My relationship with my husband is better. Ricky shows more respect to John, and I have been backing my husband more.

Interviewer: What do you remember from the sessions?

Mother: What stuck in my mind from all the sessions was how the therapist kept control of the situation. He kept us focused on what was the problem. We could see how changes happened right there and then in the session, instead of just going on and on and not resolving it.

It is possible that patient and therapist being mutually aware of the possibility of SST does speed up the therapeutic process. Most of the non-SST cases in the study required only two or three more sessions, which served primarily to follow up and secure the gains of the initial session. Yet, when therapy is longer, patients are more likely to attribute changes to the therapist or the therapy. In the cases where more therapy was provided and yet no improvement was indicated at follow-up, one could see (in retrospect) that a mismatch was created in the first session, and the attempt to correct it later did not work.

How Good Is Good?

Lack of feedback and the therapist's expectation of longer treatment contributed to many cases of SSTs perceived to be failures. In our study, we recorded both the therapists' and the patients' perception of SST. As clinicians as well as researchers, we are accustomed to viewing the patient's perception as subjective. Less often, we may consider the therapist's perception as equally subjective or even skewed. In trying to determine what works and what does not work in effective SST, we tried at the conclusion of each session to notice what was "good" or "well done" in the session. We were often wrong. The beautifully orchestrated session with Mary and her husband described in Chapter Three is a case in point.

Mary was being treated for the results of sexual abuse by her father. The therapist used an experiential ritual of breaking the bond with her father. At the end of the session, the therapist reported that "this is one of those sessions that you do once in a career. Everything I ever wanted to do as a therapist was portrayed in that session. If only I could have videotaped this session [the patient had not consented to videotaping it], I probably could retire now, travel around the world, and teach this session." Much to our surprise, however, this case turned out to be somewhat of a failure. At the follow-up, the patient hardly remembered the session. She was angry at her husband and her boss and was having a very hard time controlling her temper. The therapist, having been so pleased with the session, had failed to stay in touch with the patient, and she reported feeling unsatisfied.

This case teaches that in the first session, therapists should not try to reinvent the wheel or stir up fire and brimstone. The spectacular is seldom necessary or productive. It is often better to be a "constructive minimalist" and, rather than "uncommon therapy," (Haley, 1973), try to approach SST as "common therapy." Most of the successful SSTs we have studied do not resemble the demonstrations of master therapists in conferences or books. When I studied family therapy, I observed for three years the weekly live consultations of Salvador Minuchin, a truly remarkable master therapist. I also watched all his training tapes and edited one myself. In one instance, Minuchin saw a very difficult family. For more than an hour, he tried all the tricks he knew and danced with the family, trying to enter the system in numerous ways. Nothing worked, yet it was the best training session I ever observed. Minuchin was forced to use so many skills and techniques in one session simply because nothing worked. On the other hand, in most of the SST cases where patients reported particularly successful outcomes, the therapist appeared to have conducted a rather simple, almost dull session. In fact, in many successful SSTs, it is the patient who appears in control and sets the pace for change. Furthermore, what might be perceived by the therapist as a hopelessly bad session might hold some unexpected surprises.

Michael, a forty-year-old devout Catholic and a teacher in a local college, sought therapy for his family. The family consisted of Michael, his wife, Barbara, a thirty-nine-year-old homemaker; their fifteen-year-old daughter, Christina; and their eleven-year-old son, Mikey. On the intake questionnaire, Michael described a severe family conflict, particularly between mother and daughter. The problems had started four years earlier but had worsened in the last year. When asked how serious he felt the problem to be, Michael replied that it could possibly lead to divorce, a devastating option for a devout Catholic from a long tradition of united families.

All the family members were asked to attend the first session. Only father and daughter showed up. The therapist began the session by asking where the rest of the family was. Michael said that he had pleaded and begged with his wife to come to the session, but she had insisted that nothing could improve the situation and stated that Christina would never listen to her again. Mikey had stayed home "to keep Mom company." Christina had stated that she would not come if her mother would not, saying, "She is the main problem, not me," but had finally agreed to come when Michael said that it would be a shame for him to show up without his family and asked her to come as a personal favor to him.

During the first part of the session, while the problem was being discussed, the therapist observed how close father and daughter were. They sat in close proximity to each other. When Michael talked, Christina nodded her head in total agreement. They often turned to each other and kept eye contact, indicating much nonverbal understanding. The therapist had originally been trained in psychoanalytical theory and later in the family structural-systemic approach, and he was alarmed by this sign of cross-generational alliance and possible unresolved oedipus complex. He told Michael and Christina that without the mother and Mikey in the session, he was not very likely to be of help to them, but since they were there, they might be able to help him to understand the mother and Mikey, "so that by the end of today's session we might figure out a strategy that will motivate them to come for the next session."

Much of the hour was devoted to discussing what would make the mother feel included and a contributing part of the family. The therapist did not feel that he was getting very far, so he decided toward the end of the session to loosen up and try something else: "You know, I am a family therapist who has some off-the-wall ideas about the ways in which family members can dance with each other. My wife is a scriptwriter. Her last script was a horror film about teenagers. I have known her mostly as a rather soft and shy homemaker and a devoted mother, and I was surprised to learn that she is capable of writing a horror film." He paused for a moment and then said, "You know, maybe I did learn something from her after all. So what I am going to do now is to make up a few off-the-wall scripts about the ways your family can go from here. Since you know your family much better than I do, you will tell me which of my scripts might work for your family." They liked the idea, so the therapist started with a light and funny script in which the sister taught her younger brother how to trick their parents.

In this script, the two children sneaked out of the house in the middle of the night for a secret adventure full of surprises. Their parents caught them when they returned, but they covered up for each other and made up a story. Another script was more romantic, describing a father and mother disappearing from their house one night. The worried children called the police, who started a search. While the search was going on, the parents went to the backyard of the grandparents' house and secretly started necking in the same spot where they had first kissed each other twenty-two years earlier. A dramatic script concerned a problem between a mother and daughter that became so bad that the parents decided to send the daughter to a strict Catholic boarding school. In another script, a family's conflict led to divorce, the bewildered father never married again, the beloved daughter stayed by his side till his death, and, although she was attractive, she never married herself. Christina liked the divorce script and found it to be the best solution. The therapist was disappointed with Christina's choice, because it was his least creative script and also added to a poor prognosis. When they stood up to go, the therapist gave the father his business card and said, "When the family is ready to come for therapy as a whole, please call me, and I will see you within a week."

The therapist was so convinced by the lack of full family attendance and the close father-daughter alliance that this problem could not by any means be dealt with within a single session that he did not even mention the possibility of SST, nor did he ask Michael and Christina to sign the research consent form given all his new patients during that year. The family never called back. The follow-up call was made three months later by another team member.

Interviewer: How is your family doing now?

Father: Things have improved for us since that one session. There is less conflict, more communication, and more mutual respect, particularly between my wife and my daughter.

Interviewer: Let me ask you a couple of questions about the therapy you received here. What do you remember from the session?

Father: It was only one session with me and my daughter. The therapist was very disarming. He penetrated barriers easily. He was friendly and yet able to get to the core of things. He recommended that my daughter communicate directly with her mother instead of me being in between. He encouraged us not to come again unless the whole family is there.

Interviewer: What do you recall that was particularly helpful or harmful?

Father: It was only helpful. This therapist has a genuine concern for his patients. He didn't want to be part of the problem. He wanted only to be part of the solution. He also asked a lot of questions, and he really listened. He was smart and nonjudgmental. He was forceful only once, when he needed to be, but was candid. I was very impressed with him.

Interviewer: Did you find the single session sufficient? If you had any recommendations for improvement, what would they be?

Father: It was sufficient. The session was very well run. It couldn't be better. I have no suggestions for improvement.

Needless to say, the therapist was very flattered by that feedback and would have liked all his patients to remember him this way. Yet what is even more intriguing about the follow-up of this case is that when the interviewer asked the father what he thought had made the improvement in the family conflict possible, the patient did not attribute it to the therapist or to the session but to "more family communication, more mutual respect, and many prayers."

Seven

Attitudes That Facilitate Single-Session Therapy

In carrying on my own humble creative effort, I depend greatly on that which I do not know and upon that which I have not yet done.

— *Max Weber*

Whether a therapist considers a single session as potentially valuable and sufficient therapy or as a dropout failure is a reflection of that therapist's attitude toward the phenomenon of SST in general. SST may very well threaten some therapists' egos, their theoretical orientation, and, last but not least, their pocketbooks. Termination of therapy is traditionally explored in the psychotherapy literature as primarily the client's problem (fears of abandonment, independent-dependent conflict, transference and separation anxieties, and so on). Yet single-session encounters present a difficult challenge to therapists: they are left in the dark as to whether the patient rejected their advice or invitation for further therapy, they are unable to get rewarding feedback about how useful or helpful they were to the patient, and they receive very little or no monetary reward for their efforts. The problem is similar to that expressed by Siegel (1986, p. 21) regarding oncologists: "One problem with cancer statistics is that most self-induced cures don't get into the medical literature.

A survey of the reports on colorectal cancer found only seven such cases described between 1900 and 1966, although there have certainly been many more than that. A person who gets well when he isn't supposed to doesn't go back to his doctor. If he does, many doctors automatically assume his case was an error in diagnosis. In addition, most physicians consider such cases too 'mystical' to submit to a journal, or think they don't apply to the rest of their patients, the 'hopeless' ones."

Attitudes play a central role in all forms of psychotherapy. Evidently, therapists' attitudes are expressed in their first question in the initial session. "Please tell me about yourself" and "Today I'd like to get to know you a little bit" are rather broad inquiries for information. The session will naturally include gathering information on a broad variety of life issues. Initial questions like "What is the problem?" or "How can I help you?" communicate that the therapy is about problems and that the therapist is the helper. On the other hand, an inquiry like "Between the time you called me and coming in today, what are the changes you have noticed?" communicates the therapist's interest in spontaneous changes occurring outside the session and focuses on here-and-now changes as the main area of exploration.

Since much evidence suggests that a single session is likely to be the most common treatment duration during most professional careers, the development of more positive and productive attitudes toward SST is of crucial importance. Attitude is defined by *Webster's New Twentieth Century Dictionary of the English Language* as "1. The posture or position of a person showing or meant to show a mental state, emotion or mood. 2. The manner of acting, feeling or thinking that shows one's disposition, opinion etc." In other words, attitudes reflect the three major psychological modalities: behavior (acting), affect (feelings), and cognition (thinking). Therapists' attitudes are critical to the way they operate, think, and feel in the process of psychotherapy. This chapter reviews a few prevalent attitudes of therapists and suggests alternative ones that will help SST therapists to be more effective in their actions and more positive in their feelings about the possibility of a single-session therapy.

Viewing Each Session as a Whole

Although the need to organize one's thinking according to certain categories is understandable, it often leads one to view the first session in a fragmented way. While preconceptions or theories are necessary to making sense of all the information that is heard, therapists tend to create one kind or another of partial reality or skewed perception so that they can fit the information into one of the preexisting categories of mental disorder.

Most therapists, including myself, have been trained to view psychotherapy as a relatively long process, ranging from a few months to lifelong affairs. Human problems are often very complex, and different sciences have developed different theories about their origins and nature. Attempting to become a knowledgeable and competent therapist often leads us to a specialized and fragmented definition of our role. Viewing the first session only as a time for assessment is just one example of a fragmented attitude toward the nature of psychotherapy and the therapist's role in it. According to the stereotypes, a psychiatrist is one who gives medication, the psychologist one who does psychological testing, and the social worker one who assesses home and social environments. These prototypes and areas of specialization are often irrelevant to the clients' needs or expectations of the session. Unfortunately, there often is no correlation between the clients' needs and what they end up getting.

Viewing each and every session as a whole, complete in itself, can serve as an alternative attitude not only toward SST but toward each and every session of psychotherapy. Such a view is not necessarily more correct than the fragmented one; it is merely more useful for the treatment of SST clients. Once therapists are ready to shift from a fragmented to a holistic attitude, they can expect therapy to start right away. Furthermore, they will realize that assessment is an ongoing process that continues throughout therapy. Making interpretations or reframing the presenting problem can be therapeutic as well as diagnostic when the client's reactions are observed.

When a strike had resulted in a lack of secretarial support in our department, I once took upon myself for a few weeks the role of answering the phone and scheduling initial sessions. During this process, I realized that not only diagnostic impressions but also presession therapeutic interventions were sometimes formulated without my awareness. Today, I often prescribe to clients a therapeutic assignment under the heading of gathering information. Any therapeutic encounter is a part of a larger and longer process. One session or a hundred sessions would still be a small segment of this process. Taking each session one at a time and treating it as a whole can help the therapist to make use of the present without fearing the future. It encourages both client and therapist to do something about the problem without large expenses and dependency. It suggests that we may get more than one chance to treat our problems and that problems come and go and can be dealt with intermittently.

Is More Always Better?

The attitude that more is better serves a competitive-consumer society as well as the Judeo-Christian ethic of "trying harder." This attitude has accommodated many a therapist's journey into the depths of the human mind and provided a good and stable income for private therapists working on a fee-for-service basis. A number of clinical and theoretical notions were developed to explain the need for deeper and longer therapy. We learn, for instance, that serious therapy and lasting change can be achieved only via "deep" personality changes, that developing a therapeutic alliance is a long process that should be done cautiously, that client resistance to the therapist and to change is inevitable, that transference and countertransference have to be carefully "worked through," and that termination is a very delicate matter that the client and the therapist should take their time to work on very gradually.

Such attitudes make psychotherapy an impossible profession, in which most therapies are likely to end prematurely (at least from the therapist's point of view). In the rapid process of developmental, economic, and familial changes, many long-term psychotherapies end as a result of factors such as relocation, lack of insurance coverage, or change of jobs. I remember that after eight years of psychological training and a few years of psychotherapy for myself, I was very puzzled by the fact that most of my clients used only a few sessions to treat rather difficult problems, certainly more difficult than those that led me to seek therapy. I constantly struggled with the thought that either I had failed to create a therapeutic alliance or the patients had dropped out prematurely. This negative attitude toward myself and my clients was hardly useful. Later, I found out that the struggle to bridge the gap between in-depth training in psychology and the reality of everyday practice is very common among providers, particularly those in public services, who treat minority, welfare, or working-class populations. Groups, such as the Mental Research Institute (MRI), that treat clients in ten or fewer sessions are still considered among professionals as revolutionary. Usually, more is still considered better, and less is thought of as second-rate, superficial, and insufficient.

Another aspect of this attitude is that big problems require big solutions. It assumes that the session should begin with the notion that the client has a deep-seated problem. Since the problem was built up over many years and is rooted in early childhood, it will need a long time to be resolved. It will require extensive reparenting, uncovering, structural changes, and a long process of working through. The alternative to this attitude is not that less is always better but that small is beautiful. We want to take things one at a time, try to seize the moment, and empower the present as it is. Small changes in perception, feelings, or behavior may lead to exposure to new life circumstances, initiating new reactions by the client or his or her family members.

The advantages of adopting the attitude that a small change is sufficient are threefold: (1) It takes the pressure off both therapist and client, so neither falls over his or her feet in the process of trying too hard. (2) The client is more likely to be willing to make a small change than a big one. (3) Any kind of movement may suffice to ignite hope in the client (Rosenbaum, Hoyt, and Talmon, 1990).

Reviewing the first ten years of my psychotherapy practice, I found out that most of my therapeutic failures resulted from working too hard and saying too much. In my present therapeutic sessions, I look for the smallest, simplest step toward change. My expectation is that when my client leaves the session remembering one new point (or tries out one new behavior), it is plenty. Nevertheless, my thinking and clinical formulations are often still very complex. On the basis of my training, I might entertain multiple formulations of the present problem, ranging from dynamic to behavioral, cognitive to systemic. Yet what I communicate to the client is governed by what, at this point in time and given the client's values and view of the problem, I can say or do that will be most effective in relieving the client's stress, pain, or problem or get the client unstuck.

Psychotherapy as a Science

The idea that psychotherapy can be a science and that the therapist can take the objective view of an expert in this science clearly generated much research and scientific training of therapists, most noticeably those who take a behavioral, cognitive, or biological approach toward psychotherapy. Clients as well as therapists often have high hopes for a scientific breakthrough, and the advances in areas such as psychoneuroimmunology and biological psychiatry are indeed remarkable. The interconnectedness between the neurotransmitters in the brain, the immune mechanisms, and the psychological state of mind is well supported by research (Solomon, 1987). Most importantly, we know now that these neurotransmitters play a much greater role in both the genesis of illness and recovery from it than had previously been suspected. Despite the bad press about drugs and the crusade against all forms of them, we may anticipate that in the next decade effective and relatively safe drugs will be used not only to control the overflow of emotions such as anxiety, depression, anger, and mania but also to illicit verbal and nonverbal expressions of positive emotions ranging from happiness and love to appropriate sadness. With that knowledge, we can hope for much closer interdisciplinary efforts and more scientifically based decisions as to when to use psychotropic drugs and when to avoid them. Trying to adopt scientific ideas and attitudes toward psychotherapy, which is based on conversations over a long period of time, is often problematic. One would try to match the disorder with the treatment modalities scientifically found to be most effective. Thus, a client diagnosed as manic-depressive would be sent to a biological psychiatrist for medication, one with a phobia would be referred for behavioral treatment, and one who presents a personality disorder would be referred for psychodynamic treatment. In theory, this is the right approach and the most logical one. Reality presents a different picture:

1. The results of psychotherapy research are at best problematic. As Frank (1987) eloquently put it, "The traditional methods of exact science are ill-suited to deal with the meaning and values that provide the very stuff of psychotherapy" (p. 298).
2. Despite the efforts of therapists to apply objective diagnostic categories, factors such as context (for example, hospital or chemical dependency program) and the therapist's theoretical bias or area of specialty will often override any so-called objective measures.
3. The exceptions to the rules are as common as the rules and categories of psychopathology. Often, patients do not fit a particular diagnostic label or fit it only temporarily.

A dramatic example of the difficulty of scientific diagnosis is found in the Vermont study of 269 patients diagnosed as schizophrenics, chronic type, who failed to respond to medication (Harding and others, 1988). These patients had an average of sixteen years of illness, ten years of total disability, and six long-term hospitalizations. These early-middle-aged (average

age forty), poorly educated, lower-class individuals had been further impoverished by repeated and prolonged hospitalization. They had many peculiarities of appearance, speech, and behavior. They were touchy, suspicious, temperamental, unpredictable, unrealistic, and unable to make adequate social or practical day-to-day decisions. They also suffered a high incidence of chronic physical and psychomotor disabilities. Many were obese. Undoubtedly, this group belongs to one of the most "stable" and consistent diagnostic groups of chronic mental disorder. Yet longitudinal study following these patients for twenty-five to thirty years after their release found that 68 percent of the former schizophrenics were psychologically and socially functional, 45 percent had no signs of disability at all, and 50 percent were no longer even taking medications. Similar results were found in longitudinal studies in Europe (Harding and others, 1988). In short, what might appear in the hospital or in therapy to be a chronic condition often changes dramatically once the patient is outside the therapist's office and over a longer period of time.

In the context of SST, the alternative attitude is not to ignore scientific findings or acquired knowledge but rather to keep them in reserve while leading the session with what a Zen master would call "a beginner's mind" by following patients' struggles to solve their problems and reduce their pain and the worry. This attitude allows the therapist to be surprised and creative. It means that an important part of the therapeutic process is the humble knowledge that we do not know everything and what we do know might or might not be useful for the individual client. Therapists can assume that in nearly half of their cases, the problem will be solved spontaneously, and all that the therapist needs to do is to allow it to happen. They can also safely assume that the majority of their clients either will not follow the therapist's instructions at all or will translate them into their own language. When a therapist chooses to make use of a scientifically proven treatment or a treatment that has helped other clients, the key question is not whether this is the right treatment but rather whether this is the right timing, given the client's belief system, attitude, or hopes. Without the client's cooperation, willpower, and motivation, the most correct scientific or logical intervention will accomplish very little. In short, the therapist's aim is to be useful, not to be right. Making the "correct" diagnosis or recommending the "right" treatment is often the best way to be ineffective.

Both clients and therapists ascribe meanings to their experience. The meaning one assigns may contribute to one's difficulties. Therapists are often experts in adding heaviness and deep meanings to what might actually have been a chance fluctuation that got stuck as people put excessive unproductive energies into solving it. Most clients come to therapy in this state. They are stuck with a problem to which they feel all attempted solutions have failed. They are overwhelmed with the problem's size and view themselves or the problem in negative terms. If the therapist's attitude is to expect a small change, to provide positive attributes, and to focus instead of broaden, the therapist is more likely to induce hope and lead to workable solutions. This is a matter of approaching each hour with the openness that will best serve both therapist and patient in the pursuit of the unknown (Langs, 1979).

The Myth of Cure

"The goal of psychotherapy is to cure the patient of his or her illness." This common attitude among psychotherapists goes beyond even the medical definition of cure as removing the illness symptoms. Many therapists look for the novel goal of personality changes as a prerequisite for a real psychological cure. They argue that seeking simply a removal of symptoms will result in the substitution of new symptoms, since the basic or deep problem of the personality was not addressed. This attitude is also evidenced in psychiatric hospitals justifying long-term hospital stays. For example, a psychiatric hospital in northern California sells its services with the total treatment philosophy. The hospital promises to heal not only the psychiatric symptoms of a patient, but also those aspects of his or her life style and personality that contribute to the psychiatric disorder. In "selling" such promising packages to clients, providers set high expectations and necessitate long and expensive treatments.

Some clients, especially the psychologically minded ones, may come to treatment in order to "find themselves," "find happiness," or "find meaning to life." When therapists buy such a definition as the goal of therapy, they are likely either to fail or to see the clients reach their goal temporarily, only to find out in the next session that other problems have surfaced in the meantime. The alternative attitude might be defined as "promise less and deliver more," or as intermittent therapy, where both therapists and clients are aware that problems and symptoms are likely to come and go. Most clients arrive in therapy overwhelmed or stuck with their problems. By offering a more focused and realistic goal, therapists can help the client get back in charge while giving up unrealistic expectations of self or others.

While curing or healing a client is always a noble goal, life is a constant struggle with stress and changes. The idea that one can be cured once and for all is rather dangerous for both therapists and clients. When I was a graduate student, I received supervision from an old and wise psychoanalyst whom I deeply respected. In one of our sessions, I asked her how one determines whether psychoanalysis was indeed successful. She replied, "When a patient concludes analysis and I never hear from or see him or her again, I assume that analysis was completed successfully. If the patient keeps sending me cards for the holidays and calls me every once in a while, I know that analysis was not successful." The SST therapist needs a different attitude. Therapists approaching the single session as the one and only opportunity to cure their clients are expecting too much of themselves and may end up feeling quite anxious and overwhelmed. Cummings (1986) argued that the concept of cure has held back psychotherapy more than has any other concept. Any therapy, including SST, is likely to continue intermittently throughout one's life cycle.

If clients return to see us later on (especially if we have been helpful previously), that does not mean that we failed to cure them; it means that they used our services properly and in a timely fashion. Many of my private clients in Israel were graduates of long-term psychoanalysis. When I asked them why they did not return to their previous therapist, many of them explained that that would be as if they had failed or had had to repeat a class. Others simply said that they could not afford another long and expensive treatment, and they hoped that my more targeted treatment and commonsense approach would help them. Cummings (1986, p. 430) suggests that the therapist should offer clients the following bargain: "I will never abandon you as long as you need me. In return for that, I want you to join me in a partnership to make me obsolete as soon as possible."

The Myth of Patient Compliance

The attitude that a good patient is a compliant one, a common attitude among therapists as well as other providers, is based on the assumption that what we have to offer to the clients is better than what they can offer themselves. The psychotherapy literature is full of discussions about client resistance and noncompliance and ways to deal with their oppositional behavior. Therapists assume that if clients adopt their interpretations, take the prescribed medications, or follow the therapeutic tasks, they will get better. Recent research (as cited in Siegel, 1986, 1989) as well as patients' personal accounts (Cousins, 1979, 1983) indicate that many times the troublemakers, those who challenge the doctor, question every decision, and burst out of the hospital in anger, are more likely to survive difficult illnesses such as cancer than are the compliant and passive patients who follow doctors' instructions faithfully. Clients who examine doctors' orders and consider other alternatives present a difficult challenge to the therapist. They offer us an opportunity to expand our horizons and learn something new. They invite us to use their creativity and learn from their "doctor from within."

Clients do not follow theories or *DSM-III-R* categories. They follow their own course. Let's say a therapist calls a client who terminated before the therapist was ready and says, "Since you did not show up at our last appointment, I am calling to express my concern about your health, to find out why you did not show up, and to remind you that you are going to be charged for no-shows." The client is likely to respond like a "bad child" who was put in a corner, and the therapist will conclude that the no-show was another symptom of the client's immaturity or inability to be responsible or perhaps a sign of resistance to change. Therapists who wish to learn from their unplanned SST clients may say something like this: "Since we did not have the opportunity to meet last week, I am calling to find out how you are doing now and what you have found to be useful in solving the problem so far."

Therapy as Nurturing Birth and Growth

While my colleagues and I were finishing our sixty attempts at planned single-session therapy, my daughter Ela was born in a beautiful and natural home birth. During the process of the pregnancy and birth, I learned to look at what we did as facilitating the natural process of change, which minimizes the doctor's power and maximizes that of the patient. I found the metaphor of my role as a therapist being like that of a midwife to be very appropriate. After Ela was born and we started raising her, I got tuned again to the very long and often hard process of growing up (both my baby's and mine). Holding her, changing her diapers, caring, and simply being there became the joyful center of my life. Today, I find myself treasuring both the "magic of the moment" like that of a new birth and the very long process of growing up. I feel thankful to both long- and short-term clients for teaching me about the power of the moment as well as the mysteries of lifelong issues and our constant attempts to solve them. It seems that the argument about long- versus short-term therapy is another skewed perception invented by therapists. My own personal experience has taught me that all forms of therapy are, in a way, both long and short.

I hope that this book helps therapists to be more comfortable in crossing the orthodox lines of short- versus long-term therapy, family-system versus individual-dynamic, or behavioral versus biological toward a more integrative and practical approach—one that, instead of any pet theory, empowers clients and embraces life.

Resource A:
Follow-Up Interview

The following form was used for making the follow-up phone calls for the SST study with Michael Hoyt and Robert Rosenbaum. If the identified patient was a child, the parent that initiated the treatment was called and the same questions were asked regarding the child and family situation.

Patient: _____   Age: _____
Therapist: _____   Date of SST: _____
Date of follow-up: _____   Interviewer: _____

Identify yourself and say that you are calling for a follow-up (name therapist, date, and place of session). Make sure that the patient has the time now and is willing and available to talk freely.

1. Read to the patients verbatim their original statement of the problem or complaint. Ask: "Do you recall that?" "Is that accurate?"
2. Would you say that (restate the problem as described by patient) is about the same or has changed? (If changed, list a five-point scale from much improved (1) to much worse (5).)

3. How are you doing? (pause, open-ended question) In what way (thinking, feeling, acting) different?

4. How do people around you say you have changed?

5. What do you think made the change (for better or worse) possible? (If conditions are the same, ask, "What makes it stay the same?")

6. Besides the specific issue of (state main problem), have there been other areas that have changed (for better or worse)? If so, what?

7. Now let me ask you a couple of questions about the therapy you received. What do you remember from the session? (pause, open-ended question)

8. What do you recall that was particularly helpful or harmful?

9. How satisfied are you with the therapy you received? (List a five-point scale from very satisfied (1) to very unsatisfied (5).)

10. Did you find the single session to be sufficient? If not, was treatment continued here or elsewhere? If not, would you wish to resume treatment or change therapists?

11. If you had any recommendations for improvement, what would they be?

12. Is there anything I have not specifically asked that you would like me to know? (pause)

Thank patients for their time and participation. Remind them that they can recontact the therapist they saw at any time, or, if they desire additional services, they can call the clinic.

Resource B:
Tips for Managing
Time and Money

There are several reasons why therapists are likely to resist or largely ignore the role that SST plays in their practice:

1. The single session provides therapists with the smallest financial reward, particularly if they are in private practice or a fee-for-service setting.
2. The single session often leaves therapists with little information or knowledge about their patients.
3. The single session does not allow therapists to form a close and intimate therapeutic relationship with patients.

Money, knowledge, and intimacy are powerful forces in therapy, as they are in most aspects of life, and cannot be ignored when a therapist needs to decide whether to offer a patient more therapy. Therapists must take good care of their own needs if they are to take good care of the needs of their patients. The following are some ways in which therapists who often encounter SSTs can take care of their needs.

Money

One solution is to work on a salary base with a company that is genuinely interested in your productivity and their mem-

bers' satisfaction. Cost-effectiveness usually leads to higher satisfaction for both providers and customers. Since SST offers the
company a way to reduce waiting lists without increasing the
number of paid staff, it may increase therapists' salaries on the
basis of qualitative and quantitative criteria such as patients'
reports of improvement and level of satisfaction and how many
new patients therapists have seen at a given time. Harvard
Community Health Plan, a health maintenance organization
in Boston, offers mental health employees a partnership with
the physicians and a share of the plan's profits. Furthermore,
a therapist's income progresses according to a merit system based
on his or her patients' progress and satisfaction as well as the
therapist's effectiveness. Therapists have their own fears about
being watched or evaluated, but the days when a therapist can
get a doctorate, complete an internship, and open a successful
private practice without ever being watched will soon be over.
As in any other business providing services, therapists will have
to report regularly on the cost-effectiveness of their treatments.
By setting their own criteria and establishing a system for feedback (from patients, colleagues, or even the computer), therapists can gain more control over their pattern of practice and
at the same time improve their clinical skills and effectiveness.

If therapists practice privately and provide services to companies that deliver packages of time-limited mental health services (such as EAPs, HMOs, or PPOs), they can suggest (and
in some cases they will be offered) ways in which the purchasers
can reward therapists financially for an effective SST. A company that offers a three- to five-session assessment package
recently agreed to pay me for my time instead of paying me
the regular fixed price per regular session. This way, I was free
to use presession telephone evaluations and extended single session for the price of a number of sessions. At the end of the year,
the same company evaluated my performance and paid me a
15 percent bonus. Therapists in group practice can negotiate
with different companies a full-risk or shared-risk situation where
the therapists provide mental health services against a prepaid
fee. An example is the American Biodyne Company in San Francisco, which is owned and directed by a group of psychologists

who offer unlimited mental health services for a prepaid fixed fee. Since they are at full risk, they are financially motivated to conduct therapy as effectively (to avoid morbidity, mortality, and lawsuits) and as briefly (to maintain profits) as possible.

In direct service (with no third-party payments), therapists can set a much higher fee for a single-session consultation than for a regular session, so they can take some extra time for a thorough job of studying the case before the session, talking to other providers who were involved in the case or to the patient's family members, and conducting an extended session as well as a follow-up. Therapists should explain their plans to their patients at the outset. They may set the fee in advance or charge the same way other professionals do: logging all the time spent on the case.

In cases where therapists feel knowledgeable and confident, they might offer a flat fee per treatment instead of per session. This might keep them highly motivated to stay on target. Another system, borrowed from Milton Erickson's work (Rosen, 1982), is aimed to motivate patients. With this system, therapists say to patients something like "I am convinced that you can solve the problem soon, and there's nothing that will please me more than seeing you doing well and going on your merry way." Then they set their regular fee for the number of sessions that they estimate will be necessary and tell patients that if they find that they want more sessions than that, they will be charged for each additional session ten percent more than for the last session. Some readers may consider such an approach to be manipulative, but it can also be regarded as a way to be more flexible and creative about potential SST patients. Money is not only part of reality but also a therapeutic issue for both patients and therapists. The therapist's goal should be to find a system that will motivate patients to solve problems and maintain a healthy life-style. Patients should be motivated to find therapists who are effective and faithful to the main purpose of psychotherapy—to help patients help themselves and assume more responsibility for their behavior, thinking, and feelings.

When patients challenge an SST therapist's fees, the therapist may tell them that he or she can refer them to therapists with lower fees. But if they elect to work with the therapist, the best way for them to save a lot of money is to take care of the problem now. Indeed, SST therapy, though it can be among the highest-priced therapies per session, can also be among the cheapest per treatment. When patients do not want their insurance company or their employer finding out about their mental or family problems, the therapist might explore how much money they have set aside or are willing to spend on treatment and suggest a trial session or sessions. When the insurance plan includes a deductible of a few hundred dollars (and it usually does), therapists can tell patients that the best way to fully protect their confidentiality is to take care of the problem within a small number of sessions so that they might not even file a claim. In private practice, frequent effective SSTs will broaden the therapists' referral base and allow more patients to pay them directly, saving both sides the need to bother with insurance claims or a third party. Although this may mean keeping fewer patients for longer therapy, therapists will be able to keep only those who genuinely can benefit from working with them.

Time

In SST, it is essential not to rush the session — if you want to get somewhere fast, sometimes you need to go slowly. It is helpful in SST not to be rigid about the magical fifty-minute session. If therapists keep in mind that the first session might very well be the last, they might consider taking more time for all their first sessions. A longer first session is cost-effective if it obviates the need for additional meetings. It can often save therapists the need to tell patients that they need more time or information before they can give them feedback and avoid their being pressed by last-minute requests by patients. Therapists might take an hour and a half for individuals, two hours for a family, and two and a half to three hours for a system consultation with a network of people, such as teachers and other providers. This is usually more time than needed, but it provides the therapist with the flexibility to include in the first session activities such as reviewing lengthy medical charts or test results. There is no need to stretch the session just because a particular length of time was allocated. For therapists who have been trained in long-term therapy, conducting SST may feel like having a constant separation anxiety and a very demanding schedule, when they need "to be on their feet" so early and so quickly. Having more time now and reminding themselves and their patients that therapy can be resumed in the future may ease that pressure.

Taking Time-Outs

It is helpful for therapists to take a time-out sometime during the session, perhaps just before its conclusion. I usually take ten minutes. This time can be used to consult with colleagues, cogitate, review notes, or just take a break. The purpose of the time-out is to filter and simplify the therapeutic message or intervention. Before taking the time-out, the therapist may say something like "You shared with me today a lot of important information. I would like to take some time so I can review it carefully before responding to your question or concern." Then the therapist may restate the focal concern or question to the patient in order to make sure that they are on the same wavelength. The time-out also heightens the dramatic impact of whatever message is given after the break. Taking one or two time-outs in SST is an example of how the therapist can use different punctuations of therapeutic time to increase the therapeutic impact of a single session. The same principle can be applied to the use of time between sessions. If at the conclusion of the SST the therapist (or patient) is not sure that it has been sufficient, a longer interval than the traditional week between the first and the second sessions can be taken. This allows patients time to consolidate the gains of the session, increase their sense of independence, and allow further spontaneous improvements to take place.

Follow-Ups, Not Dropouts

When therapists follow up with all their SST patients, they gain knowledge and decrease the chances of being left in the dark about their patients' progress. If therapists are overloaded with patients, they might find it hard to be motivated to do this. In that case, they may use assistants, trainees, or even a standardized letter to keep in touch and get useful feedback from SST patients who care to respond. Therapists should never write off or underestimate any of their patients. Some SST patients can be very good sources of more referrals, especially among their friends who are reluctant to use therapy. Much of the knowledge communicated in this book was gained in short and simple follow-up phone calls (see Resource A). With proper use of the computer and advanced telephone communication, the management of much information as well as a larger case load can be quite easy. Therapists should set a time for a follow-up phone call, meeting, or letter and mark it in the calendar at the end of every initial session with a new patient. With most patients, a follow-up call can be made one to three months after the session. This is a short enough interval that patients will be able to remember the session and long enough to allow the natural course of change to take place. For whatever purpose therapists may choose to do it (research, curiosity, public relations), a brief follow-up phone call is often a therapeutic event for the patient and an eye-opening experience for the therapist. Regardless of therapists' skills, they will always have a certain percentage of unplanned SSTs with patients who terminate prematurely. Following up is the best way to resume treatment with those who truly need further therapy.

Eventually, with all the time and money in the world, it is going to be your attitude that determines how much you enjoy your SST patients and treat them effectively. The following represents a partial checklist of what I consider helpful attitudes for the SST therapist.

1. This is it.
2. View each and every session as a whole, complete in itself.
3. All you have is now.
4. It's all here.
5. Therapy starts before the first session and will continue long after it.
6. Take it one step at a time.

7. You do not have to rush or reinvent the wheel.
8. The power is in the patient.
9. Never underestimate your patient's strengths.
10. You don't have to know everything in order to be helpful.
11. Life is full of surprises.
12. Life, more than therapy, is a great teacher.
13. Time, nature, and life are great healers.
14. Expect change. It's already well under way.

References

Alexander, F. "Psychoanalytic Contributions to Short-Term Psychotherapy." In L. R. Wolberg (ed.), *Short-Term Psychotherapy*. New York: Grune & Stratton, 1965.

Alexander, F., and French, T. M. *Psychoanalytic Therapy: Principles and Application*. New York: Ronald Press, 1946.

Baekeland, F., and Lundwall, L. "Dropping Out of Treatment: A Critical Review." *Psychological Bulletin*, 1975, *82* (5), 738–783.

Bergin, A. E., and Garfield, S. L. *Handbook of Psychotherapy and Behavioral Change: An Empirical Analysis*. New York: Wiley, 1971.

Berne, E. *Principles of Group Treatment*. New York: Oxford University Press, 1966.

Bion, W. R. "Notes on Memory and Desire." *Psychoanalytic Forum*, 1967, *2*, 271–280.

Bion, W. R. *Seven Servants*. Northvale, N.J.: Aronson, 1977.

Bloom, B. L. *Changing Patterns of Psychiatric Care*. New York: Human Sciences Press, 1975.

Bloom, B. L. "Focused Single-Session Therapy: Initial Development and Evaluation." In S. H. Budman (ed.), *Forms of Brief Therapy*. New York: Guilford Press, 1981.

Breuer, J., and Freud, S. *Studies in Hysteria.* In J. Strachey (ed.), *The Complete Psychological Works of Sigmund Freud.* Vol. 2. London: Hogarth Press, 1944. (Originally published 1893.)

Cousins, N. *Anatomy of an Illness as Perceived by the Patient: Reflections on Healing and Regeneration.* New York: Norton, 1979.

Cousins, N. *The Healing Heart.* New York: Norton, 1983.

Cummings, N. A. "The Dismantling of Our Health System: Strategies for the Survival of Psychological Practice." *American Psychologist,* 1986, *41* (4), 426–431.

Cummings, N. A., and Follette, W. "Brief Psychotherapy and Medical Utilization." In H. Dörken and Associates, *The Professional Psychologist Today: New Developments in Law, Health Insurance, and Health Practice.* San Francisco: Jossey-Bass, 1976.

DeShazer, S. *Keys to Solutions in Brief Therapy.* New York: Norton, 1985.

Dodd, J. A. "A Retrospective Analysis of Variables Related to Duration of Treatment in a University Psychiatric Clinic." *Journal of Nervous and Mental Disease,* 1971, *151,* 75–85.

DuBrin, J. R., and Zastowny, T. R. "Predicting Early Attrition from Psychotherapy: An Analysis of a Large Private-Practice Cohort." *Psychotherapy,* 1988, *25* (3), 393–408.

Eliot, T. S. "Little Gidding." In *Four Quartets.* New York: Harcourt Brace Jovanovich, 1943.

Endicott, N. A., and Endicott, J. "Improvements in Untreated Psychiatric Patients." *Archives of General Psychiatry,* 1963, *9,* 575–585.

Frances, A., and Clarkin, J. F. "No Treatment as the Prescription of Choice." *Archives of General Psychiatry,* 1981, *38,* 542–545.

Frank, J. D. *Persuasion and Healing: A Comparative Study of Psychotherapy.* (Rev. ed.) New York: Shocken Books, 1974.

Frank, J. D. "Psychotherapy, Rhetoric, and Hermeneutics: Implications for Practice and Research." *Psychotherapy,* 1987, *24,* 293–302.

Freud, A. (ed.). *Letters of Sigmund Freud.* New York: Basic Books, 1960.

Garfield, S. L., and Bergin, A. E. *Handbook of Psychotherapy and Behavioral Change: An Empirical Analysis.* (2d ed.) New York: Wiley, 1978.

Gill, M. M., Newman, R., and Redlich, F. C. *The Initial Interview in Psychiatric Practice.* New York: International Universities Press, 1954.

Goulding, M. M., and Goulding, R. L. *Changing Lives Through Redecision Therapy.* New York: Grove Press, 1979.

Grotjahn, M. "Case C." In F. Alexander and T. M. French (eds.), *Psychoanalytic Therapy: Principles and Application.* New York: Ronald Press, 1946.

Gustafson, J. P. *The Complex Secret of Brief Psychotherapy.* New York: Norton, 1986.

Haley, J. *Strategies of Psychotherapy.* Orlando, Fla.: Grune & Stratton, 1963.

Haley, J. *Uncommon Therapy: The Psychiatric Techniques of Milton H. Erickson, M.D.* New York: Ballantine Books, 1973.

Haley, J. "Therapy—A New Phenomenon." In J. K. Zeig (ed.), *The Evolution of Psychotherapy.* New York: Brunner/Mazel, 1987.

Haley, J. "Conducting the First Interview." In J. Haley, *Problem-Solving Therapy.* (2nd ed.) San Francisco: Jossey-Bass, 1987.

Harding, C., and others. "The Vermont Longitudinal Study of Persons with Severe Mental Illness. I: Methodology, Study Sample, and Overall Status 32 Years Later." *American Journal of Psychiatry,* 1988, *144,* 718–726.

Hesse, H. *The Glass Bead Game.* New York: Holt, Rinehart & Winston, 1969. (Originally published 1943.)

Hoyt, M. F., Talmon, M., and Rosenbaum, R. "Sixty Attempts for Planned Single-Session Therapy." Unpublished paper, 1990.

Kaffman, M. "Single-Session Interventions in the Kibbutz Setting." Unpublished paper, 1990.

Kaplan, H. J., and Sadock, B. J. *Comprehensive Textbook of Psychiatry* (fifth ed.) Baltimore: William & Wilkins, 1989.

Knesper, D. J., Belcher, B. E., and Cross, G. J. "Preliminary Production Function Describing Change in Mental Health Status." *Medical Care,* 1987, *25* (3), 222–237.

Knesper, D. J., Pagnucco, D. J., and Wheeler, R. C. "Similarities and Differences Across Mental Health Services Providers and Practice Settings in the United States." *American Psychologist,* 1985, *40,* 1352–1369.

Kogan, L. S. "The Short-Term Case in a Family Agency. Part I. The Study Plan." *Social Casework,* 1957a, *38,* 231–238.

Kogan, L. S. "The Short-Term Case in a Family Agency. Part II. Results of Study." *Social Casework,* 1957b, *38,* 296–302.

Kogan, L. S. "The Short-Term Case in a Family Agency. Part III. Further Results and Conclusions." *Social Casework,* 1957c, *38,* 366–374.

Kojo, I. "The Mechanism of the Psychophysiological Effects of Placebo." *Medical Hypotheses,* 1989, *27,* 261–264.

Korchin, S. J. *Modern Clinical Psychology: Principles of Intervention in the Community.* New York: Basic Books, 1976.

Koss, M. P. "Length of Psychotherapy for Clients Seen in Private Practice." *Journal of Consulting and Clinical Psychology,* 1979, *47,* 210–212.

Kottler, J. A., and Blau, D. S. *The Imperfect Therapist: Learning From Failure in Therapeutic Practice.* San Francisco: Jossey-Bass, 1989.

Langs, R. *The Therapeutic Environment.* Northvale, N. J.: Aronson, 1979.

Levinson, P., and others. "Causes for the Premature Interruption of Psychotherapy by Private Patients." *American Journal of Psychiatry,* 1978, *135,* 826–830.

Levy, T. R. "The Impact of the Initial Telephone Contact on the Involvement of Couples and Families in Therapy." Unpublished doctoral dissertation, Department of Psychology, Columbia Pacific University, 1989.

Littlepage, G. E., and others. "The Problem of Early Outpatient Terminations from Community Mental Health Centers: A Problem for Whom?" *Journal of Community Psychology,* 1976, *4,* 164–167.

Lorion, R. P. "Patient and Therapist Variables in the Treatment of Low-Income Patients." *Psychological Bulletin,* 1974, *81,* 344–354.

McCord, E. "Treatment in Short-term Contacts." *The Family,* 1931, *12,* 191–193.

Madanes, C. *Strategic Family Therapy.* San Francisco: Jossey-Bass, 1981.

Malan, D., and others. "Psychodynamic Changes in Untreated Neurotic Patients, I." *British Journal of Psychiatry,* 1968, *114,* 525–551.

Malan, D., and others. "Psychodynamic Changes in Untreated Neurotic Patients, II: Apparently Genuine Improvements." *Archives of General Psychiatry,* 1975, *32,* 110–126.

Mann, J. *Time-Limited Psychotherapy.* Cambridge, Mass.: Harvard University Press, 1973.

Minuchin, S., and Fishman, H. C. *Family Therapy Techniques.* Cambridge, Mass.: Harvard University Press, 1981.

Noonan, R. J. "A Follow-up of Pretherapy Dropouts." *Journal of Community Psychology,* 1973, *1,* 43–45.

Orne, M. T. "Demand Characteristics and the Concept of Quasi-Controls." In R. Rosenthal and R. L. Rosnow (eds.), *Artifacts in Behavioral Research.* Orlando, Fla.: Academic Press, 1969.

Palmer, D., and Hampton, P. T. "Reducing Broken Appointments at Intake in a Community Mental Health Center." *Community Mental Health Journal,* 1987, *23,* 76–78.

Peck, M. S. *The Road Less Traveled: A New Psychology of Love, Traditional Values and Spiritual Growth.* New York: Simon & Schuster, 1978.

Pelletier, K. R. *Mind as Healer, Mind as Slayer.* New York: Delacorte Press, 1977.

Pelletier, K. R. *Toward a Science of Consciousness.* New York: Delacorte Press, 1978.

Reid, W. H., and Wise, M. G. *DSM-III-R Training Guide.* Washington, D.C.: American Psychiatric Association Press, 1989.

Rosen, S. *My Voice Will Go with You; The Teaching Tales of Milton H. Erickson, M.D.* New York: Norton, 1982.

Rosenbaum, R., Hoyt, M., and Talmon, M. "The Challenge of Single-Session Therapies: Creating Pivotal Moments." In R. Wells and V. Giantetti (eds.), *The Handbook of Brief Therapies.* New York: Plenum, 1990.

Sacks, O. *The Man Who Mistook His Wife for a Hat and Other Clinical Tales.* New York: Harper & Row, 1985.

Sarason, S. B. *The Making of an American Psychologist: An Auto-biography.* San Francisco: Jossey-Bass, 1988.

Saul, L. J. "On the Value of One or Two Interviews." *Psychoanalytic Quarterly,* 1951, *20,* 613.

Selvini-Palazzoli, M. "Why a Long Interval Between Sessions?" In M. Selvini (ed.), *The Work of Mara Selvini Palazzoli.* Northvale, N.J.: Aronson, 1988.

Siegel, B. S. *Love, Medicine and Miracles: Lessons Learned About Self-Healing from a Surgeon's Experience with Exceptional Patients.* New York: Harper & Row, 1986.

Siegel, B. S. *Peace, Love, and Healing: Body-Mind Communication and the Path to Self-Healing: An Exploration.* New York: Harper & Row, 1989.

Silverman, W. H., and Beech, R. P. "Are Dropouts, Dropouts?" *Journal of Community Psychology,* 1979, *7,* 236–242.

Solomon, G. "Psychoneuroimmunology: Interactions Between Central Nervous System and Immune System." *Journal of Neuroscience Research,* 1987, *18,* 1–9.

Spitzer, L., Skodol, A. E., and Williams, J.B.W. *Case Book: Diagnostic and Statistical Manual of Mental Disorders.* Washington, D.C.: American Psychiatric Association, 1988.

Spoerl, O. H. "Single Session Psychotherapy." *Diseases of the Nervous System,* 1975, *36,* 283–285.

Suzuki, S. *Zen Mind, Beginner's Mind.* New York: Weather Hill, 1970.

Watzlawick, P., Weakland, J. H., and Fisch, R. *Change: Principles of Problem Formation and Problem Resolution.* New York: Norton, 1974.

Weber, M. *Max Weber on the Methodology of the Social Sciences.* (E. Shils and T. A. Finch, trans. and eds.) Glencoe, IL: Free Press, 1946.

Whitaker, C., and Keith, D. "Symbolic-Experiential Family Therapy." In A. S. Gurman and D. P. Kriskern (eds.), *Handbook of Family Therapy.* New York: Brunner/Mazel, 1981.

Index